THE
ART
OF
WAR
GUIDE
TO
BUSINESS
LEADERSHIP

THE ART OF WAR GUIDE TO BUSINESS LEADERSHIP

DOMINIC HALE

SIRIUS

SIRIUS

This edition published in 2023 by Sirius Publishing, a division of
Arcturus Publishing Limited,
26/27 Bickels Yard, 151–153 Bermondsey Street,
London SE1 3HA

ISBN: 978-1-3988-3051-6
AD010974UK

Printed in China

Contents

Preface

The definitive text on strategy, *The Art of War*, counts Napoleon, Mao and even Paris Hilton among the long list of iconic fans who've spoken of its invaluable words of wisdom. Hailing from ancient China and held to be a blueprint for success, this quasi-Biblical set of commandments around military strategy, governance and organization promises to deliver the keys to the kingdom for those who apply its savvy insights. In modern times, its precise rhetoric has come to transcend the battlefield, with captains of industry and leaders of all kinds finding within *The Art of War*'s pages a brightly lit pathway to advantage. For here are fundamental eternal truths to inform decision-making and drive the quest for eminence across any arena in which humans compete.

So, who have we to thank for this manual on what to do and how to be, and how did they know these things?

Traditionally held to be the work of one man, Sun Tzu, later scholars have brought this into question, venturing it may be the collected works of a number of writers. However, given this pithy tome's provenance stretches back to the 6th century BCE, it comes as no surprise primary evidence to provide definitive proof either way has not been found. This writer takes the view it's the message and its application, rather than the man we are primarily interested in, and that there is little reason to doubt firstly the existence of Sun Tzu, and secondly, at the very least, his significant hand in *The Art of War*'s authorship.

PREFACE

What we can assert is that the text speaks to a multi-talented Da Vinci of their day – at one and the same time: writer, philosopher, general and strategist. Moreover, someone who appears to have held the dark and the light of their personality in perfect yin yang harmony – with neither passiveness nor pugilism in the ascendant, such that this is no ordinary military set of rules. Rather, it encompasses and seeks to channel the entire human condition.

Said to have lived in the Eastern Zhou period of ancient China, Sun Tzu, or 'Master Sun' is commonly held to have been a military theorist who came to King Helü of Wu's court and vitalized his armies, such that they were soon able to challenge rivals hitherto beyond their capabilities.

As a battlefield leader of his day, Sun Tzu would have been able to point to his many military successes by way of showcasing the efficacy of his theories. This first-hand experience informs and brings to the text an unshakeable conviction that is apparent throughout and serves to persuade the reader in the most profound fashion. That which he espouses would have been radical at time of writing and the book's confident and comprehensive commands continue to thrill some two and a half thousand years later.

It remains the case that wars of all description usually start from a rush of blood to the head, a testosterone-fuelled rage that loses sight of the broad goal and seeks to flex muscles and crush at all costs, being focused solely on asserting dominance. Sun Tzu, meanwhile, shows us a different way, a more effective way – one that prioritizes a holistic, diplomatic, strategic and psychological approach to conflict that acts to preserve resources and promotes the subjugation of one's foe without going into battle. For Westerners enchanted by its unusual expression, the Taoist tone which features throughout brings to the text – and has thus imported into Western thinking – concepts such as patience and acceptance that excite and resonate and have universal human application.

As a result, *The Art of War* has become an essential guide for every

type of leader. For US military intelligence personnel, it is required reading; for politicians the world over, looking to navigate the corridors of power, it is counsel they cannot do without; and for existing and wannabe executives, it constitutes the ultimate instruction manual on how to get ahead and stay ahead.

Since he advocates the merits of comprehensive assessing, planning, the capacity to adapt, to deploy subterfuge, and of swift execution once determined upon a course of action, Sun Tzu is often talked of in the same breath as that other master of cunning, Niccolo Machiavelli, who brought to the world his own strategic blueprint for achieving one's objectives two millennia later. Yet, there is a darkness and cruelty to Machiavelli, who believes in the inevitability of war and advocates a manipulative approach unchecked by any compass to achieve success at any cost. Sun Tzu, meanwhile, preaches a more measured approach, with action, where necessary, governed and regulated, and only justified when subordinated to the ultimate objective, whatever that may be.

Despite Sun Tzu's assured tone, it is his humility and an absence of ego that underpins his writing, and those leaders who fail to recognize this, fundamentally misunderstand the text. That C-suites have an outsized proportion of psychopaths within their ranks is not news. Yet if read and applied correctly, in *The Art of War* those bullies of the boardroom will not find an ally to support their solipsistic life view and lack of behavioural controls. Sun Tzu is for the others – the ones that want to become better leaders – the ones that want to listen, to learn and to apply their newfound knowledge.

Sun Tzu could be described as the original self-help guru – with something to say to all of us, whatever the scope of our authority or the sector in which we operate. *The Art of War*'s 13 sparkling and incisive stress-busting chapters show us how to compartmentalize, exercise restraint, choose our battles, learn when to strike and when to hold back: when and how to disrupt. It teaches us how to distinguish ourselves and

all those stakeholders we act for, and ultimately, how to be an inspiring, honourable, courageous and effective leader that can own our actions, safe in the knowledge we did all that could be expected of us.

It is small wonder that Sun Tzu's concise, clear, unwavering, no-nonsense instructions have appealed across the centuries to populists who have cherry-picked the bits that appeal in order to muddy the waters between truth and fiction. Yet, such a short-term approach that seeks to hoodwink, unsettle and divide opponents will only take one so far. It not only decidedly lacks honour, but in looking to constantly exploit immediate opportunities without planning or principle, the only outcome can be an unstable system predicated on chaos, which is ultimately unsustainable. For long-term continued success, *The Art of War* must be understood and adopted in its entirety, utilizing the complete toolbox of solutions Sun Tzu provides us with.

This book explores each chapter in turn, linking Sun Tzu's declarations to pertinent and relatable modern-day business and leadership practices and themes. For *The Art of War* has something to say on all of it. Branding, first mover advantage, networking, big data, dispute resolution, board relations, market share, M&A, customer relations, employee relations, investor relations, best practice, diversity, recruitment, and a whole lot more besides.

Sun Tzu kicks off proceedings by making it clear that hope is not a plan. Rather, one needs to take into careful, calculated consideration what may be necessary or may happen in the future, based upon the facts to hand. He moves on to illustrate how good leadership is based upon building trust and that this is an essential prerequisite to pivoting, adapting, evolving and thriving against a backdrop of continuous change. Firm but fair is the order of the day here. One must present at least the illusion of being all-knowing to maintain motivation and inspire loyalty and devotion. He reminds us it is possible, and in fact crucial, to be at one and the same time decisive, commanding and benevolent.

In chapter two, the master moves on to talk of the importance of balancing the books and of decision-making informed by the resources to hand. For Sun Tzu, it's all about facts and outcomes, and leaders that ignore these guiding lights should be considered highly irresponsible.

Chapter three brings to the fore one of *The Art of War*'s central tenets that the best fights are the ones we avoid. The key to this, according to Sun Tzu, is maintaining an even humour and resisting the malign influences of temptation and frustration that will be sure to cloud one's judgement. Here, he preaches the merits of measuredness, adaptability, patience, teamwork and a leader's capacity to act autonomously once empowered.

Chapter four talks of method, discipline and control and shows us that profound insight into the competition amounts to the 20/20 vision every leader needs. The ability to research in depth and to think outside the box are essential attributes, according to Sun Tzu. What's more, it's how you apply the resources and knowledge at your disposal that counts, understanding that a leader is an alchemist who concocts the perfect mix to transform things for the better.

Hereafter, *The Art of War* foretells the unofficial mantra of the Marine Corps in reminding us to improvise, adapt and overcome. For any leader, the landscape is ever-changing, no two battles the same. In that case, one must not be predictable. Mix it up and seek out the path of least resistance, we are told.

At its halfway point, *The Art of War* is reminding us to leave nothing to chance. Know your enemy, your marketplace, your business. Buy-in from as many stakeholders as possible connected to achieving your goals is key, with both carrot and stick needing to be used to secure it. In this way, and by remaining patient, restrained and alert at all times, a leader will be well positioned to react to the most extreme curveball – whether from within or without – with the perfectly timed and pitched response.

In the latter sections, Sun Tzu reminds us not to let our heart rule our head. Impossible tasks should be recognized as such, and left well alone,

for heroic failure is still failure. It is one thing to know the competition, but just as (if not even more) important to know yourself and those under your command. There are many wins out there and also many roads.

Here, we see it is essential to identify which prize we seek, in order to inspire around it and craft the right path to victory. And those human assets that collect around our vision must be rewarded, for the intelligence they provide gives us the insights we need to both strike upon and to deliver on our objectives with confidence.

Sun Tzu's final chapters speak to deploying logic in not making life unnecessarily difficult for oneself in pursuit of one's objectives, and in having a clear rationale for action. This does not rule out being bold, however, or marching to the beat of a different drum. The greatest leaders are intrepid and dauntless, not because they lack preservation instinct, but because they've done their homework and have faith in their ability to implement the right solution for the occasion.

Testament to its ability to transcend time and place, it may surprise some to learn that *The Art of War* also has much to say to a business world today increasingly informed by concepts such as corporate social responsibility, the fight against climate change, knowledge transfer, capacity building and philanthropy, as more enlightened interests seek to push collaboration and co-operation over conflict and domination. Can *The Art of War*'s messages sit comfortably alongside the messages marking new movements, such as 'MeToo' and 'Black Lives Matter'? The answer is a resounding yes, just as ancient religious texts still speak to us when we look past the superficial contexts of their time to the deeper meaning and message within. Perhaps then, less '*The Art of War*', than 'The Art of Achieving One's Objectives'.

So, read on, and be transported to ancient China for unadulterated business enlightenment today.

CHAPTER ONE

LAYING PLANS

1   Sun Tzu said: The art of war is of vital importance to the State.

2   It is a matter of life and death, a road either to safety or to ruin. Hence it is a subject of inquiry which can on no account be neglected.

3   The art of war, then, is governed by five constant factors, to be taken into account in one's deliberations, when seeking to determine the conditions obtaining in the field.

4   These are: (1) The Moral Law; (2) Heaven; (3) Earth; (4) The Commander; (5) Method and Discipline.

5 & 6   The Moral Law causes the people to be in complete accord with their ruler, so that they will follow him regardless of their lives, undismayed by any danger.

7   Heaven signifies night and day, cold and heat, times and seasons.

8   Earth comprises distances, great and small; danger and security; open ground and narrow passes; the chances of life and death.

9   The Commander stands for the virtues of wisdom, sincerity, benevolence, courage and strictness.

10   By Method and Discipline are to be understood the marshalling of the army in its proper subdivisions, the graduations of rank among the officers, the maintenance of roads by which supplies may reach the army, and the control of military expenditure.

11   These five heads should be familiar to every general: he who knows them will be victorious; he who knows them not will fail.

12   Therefore, in your deliberations, when seeking to determine the military conditions, let them be made the basis of a comparison, in this wise:—

13   (1) Which of the two sovereigns is imbued with the Moral Law?

(2) Which of the two generals has most ability?

(3) With whom lie the advantages derived from Heaven and Earth?

(4) On which side is Discipline most rigorously enforced?

(5) Which army is stronger?

(6) On which side are officers and men more highly trained?

(7) In which army is there the greater constancy both in reward and punishment?

14   By means of these seven considerations I can forecast victory or defeat.

15   The general that hearkens to my counsel and acts upon it, will conquer: let such a one be retained in command! The general that hearkens not to my counsel nor acts upon it, will suffer defeat:— let such a one be dismissed!

16   While heeding the profit of my counsel, avail yourself also of any helpful circumstances over and beyond the ordinary rules.

17   According as circumstances are favourable, one should modify one's plans.

18   All warfare is based on deception.

19   Hence, when able to attack, we must seem unable; when using our forces, we must seem inactive; when we are near, we must make the enemy believe we are far away; when far away, we must make him believe we are near.

20   Hold out baits to entice the enemy. Feign disorder, and crush him.

21   If he is secure at all points, be prepared for him. If he is in superior strength, evade him.

22   If your opponent is of choleric temper, seek to irritate him. Pretend to be weak, that he may grow arrogant.

23   If he is taking his ease, give him no rest. If his forces are united, separate them.

24   Attack him where he is unprepared, appear where you are not expected.

25   These military devices, leading to victory, must not be divulged beforehand.

26 Now the general who wins a battle makes many calculations in his temple ere the battle is fought. The general who loses a battle makes but few calculations beforehand. Thus do many calculations lead to victory, and few calculations to defeat: how much more no calculation at all! It is by attention to this point that I can foresee who is likely to win or lose.

Hope is Not a Plan

From almost its first words, *The Art of War* makes it abundantly clear to us that planning is everything, and we must seek 'to determine the conditions obtaining in the field'.

Simply hoping that force of will, fate, or the rehashing of old plans will allow one to deliver on objectives is a sure-fire way to fail.

Think of several short-lived crypto-moguls that got found out when their digital currency's underlying Ponzi qualities were revealed under market pressure. November 2022 marked something of a watershed moment when hordes of investors realized they'd been consumed by a get-rich-quick gold rush mentality as high-profile cryptocurrency exchange FTX and its sister trading firm Alameda Research filed for Chapter 11 bankruptcy protection.

Tethering one's fate to the untested bombast of attention-hungry maverick CEOs, like FTX's Sam Bankman-Fried, from a gut-feeling they'll be the next big thing, does not constitute a plan.

Think mobile phone manufacturer, Nokia, which failed to see the importance of software over hardware and went from market leader to being sold off in less than a decade. Its leaders could be characterized as complacent, blind to the fact that plans in place to maintain overwhelming market share were tired and redundant until it was too late to do anything about it.

Five Constant Factors

The Art of War's first chapter talks of five constant prevailing factors that must be implicitly understood in each given situation before successful plans can be made and a course of action struck upon. In the business world, this means making a detailed assessment of one's own organization – including oneself – as well as the competition, to establish strengths and weaknesses. Only by doing this, can a company or the 'State' make the necessary changes and determine when and how to strike in the marketplace.

Firstly, we hear of the 'Moral Law'. This is the cause or mission statement that serves to bind an organization together; that unites and inspires loyalty.

Without it, soldiers won't know what or who they're fighting for, nor staff on the team what their company stands for and why it exists. Successfully communicating this will imbue the soldier or worker with purpose and zeal and elevate their day to something more profound than simply turning up for a predictable pay cheque. It has been said of Apple's lionized founder Steve Jobs, 'He could make the task of designing a power supply feel like a mission from God.'

Knowing what binds, inspires and drives the competition inevitably informs one's own vision and rallying cry. It is a must know.

The second factor Sun Tzu describes as 'Heaven', which equates to the broad environment in which an organization, be it an army or a company, operates. As outlined in *The Art of War*, practically speaking, this relates to dynamics such as the time of day or year and the prevailing weather conditions, and these concerns are no less relevant for body corporate or SME (small and medium enterprise) leaders.

In the retail clothing sector, at its most basic level, this might mean ensuring winter ranges of clothes are in stores in good time for the season in question. At a slightly more complex strata, it could see a discernment

that with COVID-19-induced lockdowns coming to an end, so too would the online stampede for comfortable athleisure and casual-wear. And, at a strategic level it sees someone like Amancio Ortega, the famed Spanish billionaire former boss of clothing giant, Zara, assess that the customer and word on the street, rather than elite fashion shows, must inform his company's clothing lines, since this allows for a seamless connection between what people want and what's in store. Moreover, his belief in a high degree of control over the supply chain, centred on or near the Iberian peninsula, has allowed for swiftest-in-class responses to changing trends and a highly agile operation.

When Sun Tzu speaks of 'Earth', the third constant, he speaks of the different terrains a leader must have the measure of. For example, in the United States, out of town shopping malls experienced explosive growth after the Second World War, with savvy investors determining the commercial imperative to be best served by this development, given new mass automobile ownership and the spread of suburbia. With the central business district conversely marked by a paucity of available prime land and expensive rents, ambition and growth plans found a happy new home – at least for a while. Again, the insightful business leader was able to spot when the writing was on the wall and reallocate resources. Sun Tzu would be proud.

Beyond geography, however, there are existential dilemmas leaders must wrestle with that reflect the mental and metaphysical elements of Sun Tzu's Earth constant, as well as the physical.

Further to Russia's invasion of Ukraine, leaders in Europe representing countries reliant on Russian gas to fulfil their energy needs had to weigh up their opposition to the aggressor with the consequences to their own industrial and domestic energy security that sanctions imposed would induce, and the risk that would visit upon their own political fortunes as well as the country's wider economic welfare. Politicians had to wrestle with the question of whether national welfare

in the longer-term was better or less well served by standing up to the bully.

For while various leaders agonized over the wisdom or otherwise of biting the hand that fed them in the short term, in seeking out and securing other sources of supply and potentially catalysing investment in home-grown renewable resources, they also recognized that a period of self-imposed hardship could be a price worth paying to ultimately free themselves from being in perpetual bondage to the Russian Bear.

What those leaders needed to assess was the likelihood of securing alternative sources of supply from far-flung new suppliers with which they had little existing trading relationship to base their decisions upon; with which they were in competition from peer countries subject to the same challenges; and at a price which, when translated to the end user, was not so crippling that it caused mass civil unrest and economic and social meltdown, sucking the very lifeblood from the State. At the same time the leader had to factor in the need to fulfil their minimum obligations to maintain alliances with other friendly forces, so preventing them from being isolated and losing their voice at the top table, and thereby their ability to influence dynamics at the widest possible level.

Such is the life of a general.

When speaking of the 'Commander', *The Art of War* reminds us it is a fine path the leader treads to inspire loyalty, respect and devotion.

At first glance, the virtues of wisdom, sincerity, benevolence, courage and strictness may seem a rather mixed and incompatible bag, but Sun Tzu is right in saying each is needed to ensure a leader can become the complete package. Firm but fair is the order of the day here, which means there's no place for bullies or micromanagers. Rather, a true visionary embodies the company ethos and sets the tone from the top down for the whole company, effected in the way they converse with and act

towards their subordinates. Communicate this badly, or not at all, and you are delegating malfunction. This will surely fester, grow and breed resentment, so that it not only comes home to roost personally, but also adversely impacts the organization's fortunes.

This ties in with Sun Tzu's fifth constant, method and discipline, which speaks to leading by example, which in turn makes for effective internal and external communications and creates the conditions for a fiscally responsible organization.

Yet, sleaze-mired egomaniacs like Harvey Weinstein at The Weinstein Company saw to it that the outfits they headed up were fuelled instead by the cult of their own personalities. So, when things went south and those commanders were found wanting, it soon became apparent how sandy and weak these unilateral, despotic strategic foundations were. Get the message and its delivery right, however, and see it permeate your organization, and you empower others to fight the operational fires in allegiance to the cause and in keeping with the law of the land with all the necessary tools at their disposal.

It's worth remembering that while you may be the boss, officially tasked perhaps by yourself or others in rarefied circles, your informal licence to operate comes from those seemingly beneath you.

Being a leader is a work in progress and the best ones know that continuous self-improvement and self-discipline are key. Virtuousness, as Sun Tzu sees it, can today be developed through learning and practice away from the battlefield – at business school, on the job, or via life coaching. Be the leader Sun Tzu wants us to be!

Knowing these five constants will mean one has crossed all 't's and dotted all 'i's, so making for the best laid plans; a personally enriching and intellectually stimulating exercise in itself, which can then be modified as necessary in keeping with the shifting sands of circumstance.

This Isn't the Movies

When he says, 'Which army is stronger', and 'If he is in superior strength, evade him', Sun Tzu reminds us that one must never lock horns with competitors for the sake of it. Rather, we must only go into battle with a clearly stated rationale that serves to make more secure and strengthen that which we are charged to nurture, nourish and protect. If that means biding one's time and no war today, so be it. Headstrong decisions and actions usually lead to defeat, and while the movies might like to attach glory to Spartacus-style heroic failure, shareholders, staff, customers et al are rather less forgiving when a business leader gets it wrong.

The efforts of Japanese video game multinational, Nintendo, to steal a march on the new dawn that was virtual reality back in the 1990s should make us mindful. Its 1995-released 'Virtual Boy' was a notorious commercial flop. Rushed out with a lack of clear leadership in a quest to be synonymous with this new tech by securing first mover advantage, this head-mounted console became a byword for how not to do it.

Marked by technology that was not fit for purpose, underwhelming effects and a high initial price that was then repeatedly slashed, its travails were further compounded by health concerns and an ill-conceived promotional campaign that inexplicably sought to shift Nintendo away from its proven core child market. Finger-pointing ensued, and the resulting negative brand association ended up costing Nintendo a place at the VR top table, a state of affairs which continues today.

Had the iconic video game company kept its cards closer to its chest, things could have been so different. Yet, its belief in its own Midas touch got the better of it on this occasion and caused it to be over-transparent. As *The Art of War* makes abundantly clear in the latter passages of chapter one, 'all warfare is based on deception', while 'the devices leading to victory must not be divulged beforehand'.

Nintendo's unenviable legacy could have been avoided with stronger

risk management processes, more exhaustive R&D and the identification of a clear raison d'être for the product. The company was lucky to get away with it, for high profile failed releases born from a lack of analysis can be catastrophic for companies, even of its renown. Just think of Sega, which was compelled to exit the console market altogether as it attempted unsuccessfully to square up to Sony's PlayStation in all the wrong ways. Maybe Sega's senior leadership hadn't read *The Art of War*, for if they had, they would have noted, 'It is as a matter of life and death, a road either to safety or to ruin.'

Update or Die

Where Sun Tzu's plans involved first assessing his military foes' capabilities and likely actions, today's business leader must study the market to develop the best means of developing advantage for the benefit of those stakeholders on whose behalf they toil. Once clear objectives have been set, a course of action must be determined upon based on current and future conditions. Anything that acts to introduce additional insights into said conditions is to be welcomed, for sometimes the edge this affords is the difference between success and failure.

For example, the digital revolution means critical information can now be extracted from a sea of almost infinite data in lightning-quick fashion. This is acting to deliver never before seen trading enlightenment, and with it, the capacity to make swift trades with a greater degree of confidence. As Sun Tzu puts it, 'Thus do many calculations lead to victory, and few calculations to defeat.'

CHAPTER TWO

WAGING WAR

1 Sun Tzu said: In the operations of war, where there are in the field a thousand swift chariots, as many heavy chariots, and a hundred thousand mail-clad soldiers, with provisions enough to carry them a thousand li*, the expenditure at home and at the front, including entertainment of guests, small items such as glue and paint, and sums spent on chariots and armour, will reach the total of a thousand ounces of silver per day. Such is the cost of raising an army of 100,000 men.

2 When you engage in actual fighting, if victory is long in coming, then men's weapons will grow dull and their ardour will be damped. If you lay siege to a town, you will exhaust your strength.

3 Again, if the campaign is protracted, the resources of the State will not be equal to the strain.

4   Now, when your weapons are dulled, your ardour damped, your strength exhausted and your treasure spent, other chieftains will spring up to take advantage of your extremity. Then no man, however wise, will be able to avert the consequences that must ensue.

5   Thus, though we have heard of stupid haste in war, cleverness has never been seen associated with long delays.

6   There is no instance of a country having benefited from prolonged warfare.

7   It is only one who is thoroughly acquainted with the evils of war that can thoroughly understand the profitable way of carrying it on.

8   The skilful soldier does not raise a second levy, neither are his supply-wagons loaded more than twice.

9   Bring war material with you from home, but forage on the enemy. Thus the army will have food enough for its needs.

10   Poverty of the State Exchequer causes an army to be maintained by contributions from a distance. Contributing to maintain an army at a distance causes the people to be impoverished.

11   On the other hand, the proximity of an army causes prices to go up; and high prices cause the people's substance to be drained away.

12   When their substance is drained away, the peasantry will be afflicted by heavy exactions.

13 & 14   With this loss of substance and exhaustion of strength, the homes of the people will be stripped bare, and three-tenths of their income will be dissipated; & 14 while government expenses for broken chariots, worn-out horses, breast-plates and helmets, bows and arrows, spears and shields, protective mantles, draught-oxen and heavy wagons, will amount to four-tenths of its total revenue.

15   Hence a wise general makes a point of foraging on the enemy. One cartload of the enemy's provisions is equivalent to twenty of one's own, and likewise a single picul** of his provender is equivalent to twenty from one's own store.

16   Now in order to kill the enemy, our men must be roused to anger; that there may be advantage from defeating the enemy, they must have their rewards.

17   Therefore in chariot fighting, when ten or more chariots have been taken, those should be rewarded who took the first. Our own flags should be substituted for those of the enemy, and

the chariots mingled and used in conjunction with ours. The captured soldiers should be kindly treated and kept.

18 This is called using the conquered foe to augment one's own strength.

19 In war, then, let your great object be victory, not lengthy campaigns.

20 Thus it may be known that the leader of armies is the arbiter of the people's fate, the man on whom it depends whether the nation shall be in peace or in peril.

* One li is equal to 0.5 km (0.3 miles).

** One picul weighs approximately 60 kg (132 lb).

Conflict costs

In chapter two, Sun Tzu makes it clear that wars are costly affairs. If there's nothing for it but to lock horns, make sure the action is brought to a conclusion as swiftly as possible, he instructs.

'If the campaign is protracted, the resources of the State will not be equal to the strain,' says the supreme strategist.

If there were no limits on what one could throw at something to achieve one's goal, no cost too great, then victory in whichever form sought, would inexorably be achieved.

Yet infinite resources are just as much a pipe dream in business today as they were on the battlefield back in Sun Tzu's time.

Live in the Real World

Resources are finite and must be applied sparingly. Pre-eminence that cannot be sustained is pointless, and sooner or later a company, government or citizen that consistently pays no attention to balancing the books will eventually meet catastrophe as the credit dries up and the debts are called in. For example, a large staff to cover all areas with a little bit to spare just in case is a 'nice to have', but a huge overhead to carry and a deeply inefficient way of operating.

It is why late 2022 and early 2023 saw a raft of tech layoffs, as firms across the spectrum numbering among their ranks companies as disparate as computer giant, Dell, and cryptocurrency platform, Coinbase wrestled with the ravages wrought by reduced revenues and higher costs. For these two and many others besides, it was an efficiency drive deemed regrettable, but necessary, and while inevitably unpopular with many, the job cuts spoke to leaders able to acknowledge market realities and respond appropriately.

In keeping with Sun Tzu's stated objective for the goal to be 'victory, not lengthy campaigns', just like on the battlefield, businesses need to be cognizant of their exit strategy when seeking to gain market share, since a price war race to the bottom can quickly drain resources if it drags on. And even if objectives are realized, if the coffers had to be emptied to achieve that goal, it amounts to little more than a pyrrhic victory that serves to retard longer-term progress.

As a business you need to speculate to accumulate, because the competition isn't just going to roll over and hand you its custom on a plate. To convince the market that what you have is worth it is going to cost, so be sure which companies you pick fights with and that these are fights you can win with the resources to hand.

Old Hands

Chapter two also makes it clear to us that an experienced management team with knowledge of the industry at hand is essential, for it will have seen first-hand the disastrous financial consequences that must ensue from decisions informed by glory-seeking for glory's sake rather than those born of clinical analysis.

So, when Sun Tzu says 'It is only one who is thoroughly acquainted with the evils of war that can thoroughly understand the profitable way

of carrying it on,' we can apply this directly to today's business world and know that it is only the seasoned campaigner who will be able to exercise the necessary restraint and financial discipline when all around the unpractised are losing their heads, operating impulsively and instinctively with the misplaced confidence only those who have not yet tasted failure can have.

And remember, the wisest heads will know that just because a battle went well last time, it doesn't mean the dynamics are going to be the same the second time around.

TV show revivals exemplify the dangers of trying to replicate the magic of yesteryear. In such instances, commissioning parties mistakenly identify nostalgic goodwill surrounding the original as constituting an easy winning formula guaranteed to make any relaunched version a hit with audiences.

However, it rarely works out that way.

Not only is there collective amnesia that the show was cancelled first time around due to falling ratings, suggesting inherently insufficient viewer appetite, but years later, the original cast are often unavailable or uninterested, certainly older, and quite possibly, dead, bringing with it the need to quickly build up affection for a new cast. Moreover, society's attitudes and sensibilities shift, so that what makes 'good TV' today will be markedly different from the formulas that marked previous eras. This is especially evident in what audiences find funny from one decade to the next, or even consider to be acceptable humour.

The consequence of this is that most relaunches end up being either conspicuously anachronistic, or half-baked compromises desperate not to offend. The TV graveyard is littered with these soulless pastiches of original versions. Think: *Beverly Hills, 90210*; *Dallas*; *Melrose Place*; *Prison Break*; *Murphy Brown*. The list goes on.

Whatever the product or service, companies would do well to understand that each time they release something new, the market

dynamics will have shifted and new approaches – even subtle ones – can sometimes make all the difference when it comes to achieving success.

Safeguarding Supplies

Chapter two of *The Art of War* also speaks to the merits of absorbing assets from the conquered foe into one's ranks. The takeaway today is that when resources are scarce, companies have to think wisely about how to safeguard their supply chain. Just think of the electric vehicle (EV) sector which worldwide is receiving significant governmental support and incentives in the quest to catalyse the shift from conventional vehicles as part of the transition to net zero. Yet with insufficient supply of the critical minerals such as lithium, cobalt and nickel needed for the construction of the batteries, the rollout of EVs is not what it could be to meet demand. Carmakers such as Tesla, GM and Ford are actively looking at vertical integration in the form of direct ownership of mines to increase and safeguard supplies and to exert greater control over costs.

Equally, a supply chain brought closer to home in the form of onshoring, as opposed to offshoring, increases certainty, stability and predictability of supply. The possibility of extreme events such as wars, hyper-inflation or pandemics must be factored into planning, and business models stress-tested accordingly. The early 2020s evidenced such discombobulating phenomena can occur in parallel, with the result that transporting anything long distance became both hugely expensive and unreliable for companies which had to then navigate the resultant delays to orders, inability to fulfil new orders and reputational damage. As Sun Tzu remarks, 'Contributing to maintain an army at a distance causes the people to be impoverished.'

Sun Tzu's focus on chariots, helmets, spears, wagons and other battle kit speaks to resource management, and this extends to people, in that

you need adequate provisions of top talent to prosper. While in his day, there was little need to be mindful of ethical or legal considerations in how one acquired such resources, what we can extract and apply is that it's important to be proactive when seeking to attract the best people, and to incentivize accordingly, since such folk are the lifeblood of any business.

In fact, Sun Tzu reminds us that incentivization is key to keeping morale up and the soldiers – or equally, the workforce – happy and hungry for more, 'that there may be advantage from defeating the enemy.'

Performance-related bonuses would appear to have had the same allure two and a half thousand years ago as today.

The Power of Kindness

Sun Tzu wastes no opportunity to reinforce the merits of swift and decisive warfare, rather than long-drawn-out conflict. And of being firm but fair, advocating that 'the captured soldiers be kindly treated and kept.'

Sun Tzu knew that what goes around comes around, and that the economic case for creating a festering sense of resentment and desire for revenge on the part of one's enemy is hard to argue.

Had Russian President Vladimir Putin dusted off his copy of *The Art of War*, he might have thought better of weighing into Ukraine. His hoped-for quick win soon descended into the stuff of nightmares – a war of attrition with no end in sight that led Russia to become a global pariah, its economy in meltdown, and the country's unfortunate citizens seemingly tied to supporting a lost cause because the man at the top – egged on by war hawks – couldn't admit he got it wrong.

It's impossible to sustain morale in a protracted fight, with reports suggesting the morale of ill-equipped Russian troops was at an all-time

low, as they came to realize they would not be welcomed as liberators, but instead, despised as invaders, and that there was every chance of them dying on the front line for a questionable cause. As the ancient master rightly points out, the likes of Putin are those 'on whom it depends whether the nation shall be in peace or in peril.'

And while it is not impossible for dictators to keep in power as war drags on – think of Assad in Syria – in business it is harder for despotic management to prosper, since the market that sustains them cannot be browbeaten into submission.

Live and Die by Results

CEOs take note. Belligerence is not what you want you or your company to be known for. The board, shareholders, customers et al want you to be focused on driving value and growth, and if they sense your focus is elsewhere, this can impact revenue growth, revenue per client, profit margin, client retention rate, and customer satisfaction – and not in the way you want these to.

Results and focus matter. So long as a boorish autocratic leader is delivering good results, all is forgiven – but if the company they head up and are synonymous with starts to flounder, and the applied remedies only serve to compound the problem, resistance will develop and harden to a critical mass, and at this point even the most fawning acolytes will transfer their allegiances to the next company saviour waiting in the wings, especially if they see their own prospects are tied to the waning performance of the company.

When the turnover falls and the revenues dry up, there's less money to appease shareholders or to keep staff on, and disgruntled investors or employees worried about job security are only so forgiving. And just

as 'the peasantry was afflicted by heavy exactions' in Sun Tzu's time, so those that bankroll the corporate armies of today will begin to withdraw their support if dissatisfied with performance.

With so many platforms and interfaces for dissent to foment these days, seeking to clamp down and control the chatter is not an option for the troubled business manager, so that at this stage they're usually already a dead man/woman walking. And as Sun Tzu explains, 'other chieftains will spring up to take advantage of your extremity.'

In a way that transcends time and place, money was and remains king. If it's in short supply, people start to count the dollars and the cents. It is why discount retailers do so well during cost-of-living crises. Companies that fail to adapt at such times will likely haemorrhage custom, just as in Sun Tzu's day high prices caused 'the people's substance to be drained away.'

Sun Tzu leaves us under no illusion then that war does not come cheap and if we want it to enhance our lot rather than add to our woes, best make sure it's a quick quarrel.

In business, lightning-fast wins can be achieved with few inputs or the need to redirect budgets already allocated. For example, there is nothing inconsistent between acknowledging challenges and reminding stakeholders of reasons to be cheerful amid tough times. By alluding to a bright new dawn tomorrow, today's unwelcome data or news can be made more palatable, and the necessary buy-in secured for the leader's approach to overcoming current adversities.

For new leaders especially, it's all in the presentation. Even if much of the groundwork was done prior to their arrival, aligning themselves with an upward trajectory and palpable and positive change to come can be a highly effective tool with which to galvanize support.

Picking a Fight with the Wrong Guy

Internet colossus Mark Zuckerberg intimating that Facebook constituted a quasi-government did not go down well with the real US government. The provocative chat spoke to over-confidence and not a little megalomania – the logical conclusion of no one being bold enough to challenge the general's authority or question their judgement. It brought the company additional unwanted scrutiny and an ever-increasing clamour for it to be broken up, with concerns about monopolization, privacy and data protection being cited.

The Facebook CEO came to realize that governments in stable jurisdictions like the US will invariably shoot down the grand ambitions of even the biggest corporates and their leaders, like him, who believe they are 'more than'.

Being compelled to publicly defend your actions to lawmakers is not good for a company's reputation, and while not forced to offload any WhatsApps or Instagrams, Facebook parent company Meta's share price nosedived and will remain in the doldrums as long as it is mired in this long-drawn-out controversy.

This can be chalked up as a costly loss thanks to picking a fight with the wrong guy – in this case the US government, where victory would have amounted to the US government relinquishing its authority to a corporate. Hardly an outcome that could ever arrive quickly or cheaply.

Elon Musk is another example of a modern-day general who had to accept even his legendary reputation for protracted bamboozling could not defeat the law of the land that bound him to purchase Twitter at an inflated price of his own making. Loose talk costs money, he discovered.

Zuckerberg and Musk should have listened to Sun Tzu. He knew no one should bite off more than they could chew.

CHAPTER THREE

ATTACK BY STRATAGEM

謀攻

1   Sun Tzu said: In the practical art of war, the best thing of all is to take the enemy's country whole and intact; to shatter and destroy it is not so good. So, too, it is better to recapture an army entire than to destroy it, to capture a regiment, a detachment or a company entire than to destroy them.

2   Hence to fight and conquer in all your battles is not supreme excellence; supreme excellence consists in breaking the enemy's resistance without fighting.

3   Thus the highest form of generalship is to balk the enemy's plans; the next best is to prevent the junction of the enemy's forces; the next in order is to attack the enemy's army in the field; and the worst policy of all is to besiege walled cities.

4   The rule is, not to besiege walled cities if it can possibly be avoided. The preparation of mantlets, movable shelters, and various implements of war, will take up three whole months; and the piling up of mounds against the walls will take three months more.

5   The general, unable to control his irritation, will launch his men to the assault like swarming ants, with the result that one-third of his men are slain, while the town still remains untaken. Such are the disastrous effects of a siege.

6   Therefore the skilful leader subdues the enemy's troops without any fighting; he captures their cities without laying siege to them; he overthrows their kingdom without lengthy operations in the field.

7   With his forces intact he will dispute the mastery of the Empire, and thus, without losing a man, his triumph will be complete. This is the method of attacking by stratagem.

8   It is the rule in war, if our forces are ten to the enemy's one, to surround him; if five to one, to attack him; if twice as numerous, to divide our army into two.

9   If equally matched, we can offer battle; if slightly inferior in numbers, we can avoid the enemy; if quite unequal in every way, we can flee from him.

10   Hence, though an obstinate fight may be made by a small force, in the end it must be captured by the larger force.

11   Now the general is the bulwark of the State; if the bulwark is complete at all points, the State will be strong; if the bulwark is defective, the State will be weak.

12   There are three ways in which a ruler can bring misfortune upon his army:—

13   (1) By commanding the army to advance or to retreat, being ignorant of the fact that it cannot obey. This is called hobbling the army.

14   (2) By attempting to govern an army in the same way as he administers a kingdom, being ignorant of the conditions which obtain in an army. This causes restlessness in the soldiers' minds.

15   (3) By employing the officers of his army without discrimination, through ignorance of the military principle of adaptation to circumstances. This shakes the confidence of the soldiers.

16   But when the army is restless and distrustful, trouble is sure to come from the other feudal princes. This is simply bringing anarchy into the army, and flinging victory away.

17   Thus we may know that there are five essentials for victory:

(1) He will win who knows when to fight and when not to fight.

(2) He will win who knows how to handle both superior and inferior forces.

(3) He will win whose army is animated by the same spirit throughout all its ranks.

(4) He will win who, prepared himself, waits to take the enemy unprepared.

(5) He will win who has military capacity and is not interfered with by the sovereign.

18   Hence the saying: If you know the enemy and know yourself, you need not fear the result of a hundred battles. If you know yourself but not the enemy, for every victory gained you will also suffer a defeat. If you know neither the enemy nor yourself, you will succumb in every battle.

The Best Fights
are the Ones We Avoid

Chapter three of *The Art of War* sees Sun Tzu advocating the merits of applying brain over brawn in dispute resolution. As we have established, the costs of conflict are many and profound, so all avenues to achieve one's objectives without resorting to it should be explored, since this will act to preserve resources.

For business leaders, this means clear communication of responsibilities, targets, capabilities and expectations within an organization, so there's no room for doubt or misunderstanding that can lead to festering and contagious resentment. It means engaging in dialogue with customers, both existing and prospective, utilizing all the myriad channels now at companies' disposal to present a coherent vision that leaves nothing to the imagination as to what can be delivered and what it means to be part of the tribe. If by making a case with clarity and charm, targets make a beeline for one's company, rather than having to wrestle for their business, this constitutes an optimum outcome.

Some believe playing hardball is the way to get on in business. Sun Tzu would disagree. As he says, 'supreme excellence consists in breaking the enemy's resistance without fighting.'

Whether it's over-aggressive marketing techniques, browbeating employees into submission, failing to deliver on deliberately ambiguous

commitments, or muscling in on the competition, Sun Tzu would argue that acting rough and ruthless or ignobly – particularly in these more sensitive times we now live in – has every chance of alienating and antagonizing. This will ensure it takes longer and costs more to achieve one's goals – which is an inefficient way of operating.

And when injustice is seen to have taken place, whether real or perceived, the spectre of litigation comes into play – a hugely time-consuming and expensive exercise that is also potentially damaging to a firm's reputation.

While sometimes the legal route is unavoidable and actions or conduct must be defended, or challenges made to protect one's interests, an opportunity to settle out of court usually constitutes the wisest path to take. While it may lack glory and the capacity to generate headlines, glory-chasing does not pay the bills. And as for the adage that there's no such thing as bad publicity, well, that's just nonsense. Bottom line: the best leaders will see people willingly follow them and position the company so that business is drawn to it.

Make it Friendly, Not Hostile

When one company covets another, it will attempt a takeover to acquire the intended target. This can be hostile or friendly. Looked at through a Sun Tzu lens, friendly is where the win lies.

Whether it's via proxy votes, tender offers or a large stock purchase, a hostile takeover can be costly and time-consuming, whereas a friendly takeover will see the welcome mat laid out, it having been determined that this development will benefit both parties. In the latter case, the path to the desired outcome is often smooth, whereas hostile incursions are likely to meet with stiff resistance and can drag on, marked by multiple obstacles and no guarantees of success.

The Art of War would have it that a hostile takeover should be avoided, since there are so many imponderables for an accurate prediction of the outcome, and in a counter-productive move, you are likely to be weakening the very asset you seek to hold; an asset which is diverting resources to defend its independence. Sun Tzu tells us at the outset of chapter three that 'the best thing of all is to take the enemy's country whole and intact; to shatter and destroy it is not so good.'

Moreover, advisory and regulatory fees can quickly mount up, not to mention the potential for the acquiring party to be saddled with debt even if they are successful, thanks to the armoury of weapons the target may bring to bear to thwart the takeover. In addition, while the machinations run their course an air of uncertainty will inevitably hang like a pall over the target company, such that the incumbent talent underpinning the very success that brought it within the potential acquirer's sights, may jump ship for a more certain future elsewhere. In that case, the unwanted suitor will not have 'taken the enemy's country whole and intact.'

Yet, pride before a fall determines the more pugilistic-minded business leader is incapable of backing down, seeing failure to deliver on an objective as a negative reflection on their capacity to lead effectively, when in truth the opposite is true. For when the evidence suggests dogged persistence serves for the stakeholders – in whose best interests the leader is charged to act – no good purpose, it's time to withdraw. As Sun Tzu makes clear, 'the rule is not to besiege walled cities if it can be possibly avoided.'

Meanwhile, those without perspective can let the power they wield go to their heads, forgetting that their authority is bestowed and can be withdrawn – either from within or without. Like the general on the battlefield, they are but servants to the cause – albeit very well-paid heads of the household staff. As *The Art of War* explains, misfortune is not far away if one seeks to govern an army in the same way one would administer a kingdom.

Furthermore, any business decisions that are driven by stress and emotional instability, rather than cool-headed dispassionate scrutiny, are to be avoided. It is well documented that stress alters brain chemistry, and so when the brain is in a toxic stress state, it can be difficult to undertake effective cost-benefit analysis. In his own way, Sun Tzu recognized this, stating that, 'The general, unable to control his irritation, will launch his men to the assault like swarming ants.'

Those action-hero business leaders pre-programmed to scrap it out as a way to force an outcome without first weighing up the consequences will – sooner or later – fail.

So long as it is not deemed to violate competition laws by the relevant regulators – and a good leader should have overseen the relevant due diligence on this front to make the right call – a friendly takeover where the company's management and board of directors actively consent to, approve and help implement the proposal, is the preferred way to proceed. This is effectively seeing 'the skilful leader subdue the enemy's troops without any fighting (or) lengthy operations in the field.'

Think 'persuasion' rather than 'subjugation', because having people onside makes achieving one's goals an order of magnitude easier.

This doesn't mean to say there aren't numerous non-confrontational routes to the promised land. If it means coaxing, manoeuvring, cajoling or wheedling to get where you want and need to be, this is better than resorting to taking the gloves off.

Deep Pockets

In this chapter, *The Art of War* also reminds us it is essential to have the full measure of the resources available to you to scale ambitions accordingly. To take on the big boys requires deep pockets. Think of the US presidential election process where a bulging war chest of campaign

donations is required for anyone wanting to see their hat thrown and stay in the ring.

While spending the most will not necessarily deliver the keys to the White House, if you don't spend – and spend big – you won't get the media attention, nor be able to adequately fund the campaign expenses to even get out of the blocks.

To observers from other electorates around the world – where such matters can be more evenly regulated – it all sounds rather undemocratic. But it is what it is, and for Sun Tzu, being cognizant of the realities on the ground in any given situation is key. Hence he says, 'though an obstinate fight may be made by a small force, in the end it must be captured by the larger force.'

The Complete Leader

For Sun Tzu's general, read today's CEO. They must be the complete package and their competency or otherwise will determine the fortunes of the company they lead. Enlightened decision-making at the top will see the firm flourish and prosper, while headstrong resolutions will work to weaken the organization. Sun Tzu knew on the battlefield that the general of the army was the bulwark of the State that needed to be complete at all points for the State to remain strong. And so it is today.

Being the leader is no small or easy task. It is a challenging position that demands to be filled by only the most able and accomplished possessing multiple skill sets. Occupying the role is, of itself, neither a mark nor guarantee of success, however, since a leader that falls short in certain areas can put a serious dent in a company's fortunes.

Uber co-founder and former CEO, Travis Kalanick's bold disruptive shake-up of the taxi industry was impressive, and the company's rapid growth was underpinned by his lack of respect for the rules. While this

punt on launching services in advance of ticking all the regulatory boxes paid off, in that the service swiftly won the hearts, minds and wallets of a critical mass to became irreversibly established, that same gung-ho attitude also saw an unethical corporate culture take hold on his watch.

Whether it was employees, drivers, customers, competitors or regulators, Kalanick essentially shot from the hip and did as he pleased. Combined with a misreading of the Chinese market, where the service's launch failed to take off, the Silicon Valley hotshot's Midas touch deserted him, and this did not go unnoticed.

At the heart of Kalanick's downfall was a desperately poor understanding of society's changing mores and attitudes that saw misogyny allowed to prevail unchecked at the company. It was his inability to effectively respond to accusations of sexual harassment at the company that ultimately did it for him, the scathing independent report that followed compelling him to resign in 2017. Uber's top management knew, just as Sun Tzu knew, that, 'if the bulwark is defective, the State will be weak.'

The ability to adapt to circumstances to avert damaging flashpoints and to acknowledge that strategies are dependent on the appropriate resources being available for them to be implemented effectively is an essential leadership attribute.

Instructing and expecting a team to deliver the impossible 'shakes the confidence of the soldiers' and is akin to 'hobbling the army'. Such unreasonable expectations that place front-line staff in the firing line serve to erode trust in the organization and are sure to create fertile conditions for dissent within the ranks and higher turnover of staff. This will result in a leader's authority and position coming under threat from within – and also from without, courtesy of disgruntled customers' dissatisfaction with lack of delivery on what can be traced back to over-commitments set at the top. There is little more demoralizing than being set up to fail.

The takeaway here is that a one-size-fits-all approach never works. Leaders must be nimble, agile, flexible; able to pivot and adapt to ensure the right solutions for the relevant situation. And to afford the greatest scope to strike the right rational note every time, and so ensure one's corporate 'army is animated by the same spirit throughout all its ranks', a leader can and should lean on hard data to assist in decision-making. Such dispassionate source material is an essential part of the mix in helping to do away with personality politics and confirmation bias, providing critical insights and firepower at the fingertips that can be shared in real time with any relevant personnel to bring collective clarity and reduce disputes.

Ultimately, executive authority resides with the leader, and it is important they are not hamstrung by interference from other quarters, and that they are given the autonomy to strategize as they see fit. If they have been tasked with the role, it is only right they are unfettered in their capacity to discharge their duties. As *The Art of War* makes clear, 'he will win who has military capacity and is not interfered with by the sovereign.'

Sun Tzu rounds off chapter three by succinctly reminding us that advantage lies in knowing both yourself and the enemy. A leader that knows not only their own strengths and weaknesses and those of the organization they lead, but also the nature of the competition, the market and an awareness of multiple dynamics and influences, will know when to strike and when to hold back. Just like the master says, 'if you know the enemy and know yourself, you need not fear the result of a hundred battles.'

CHAPTER FOUR

TACTICAL DISPOSITIONS

1 Sun Tzu said: The good fighters of old first put themselves beyond the possibility of defeat, and then waited for an opportunity of defeating the enemy.

2 To secure ourselves against defeat lies in our own hands, but the opportunity of defeating the enemy is provided by the enemy himself.

3 Thus the good fighter is able to secure himself against defeat, but cannot make certain of defeating the enemy.

4 Hence the saying: One may know how to conquer without being able to do it.

5 Security against defeat implies defensive tactics; ability to defeat the enemy means taking the offensive.

6 Standing on the defensive indicates insufficient strength; attacking, a superabundance of strength.

7 The general who is skilled in defence hides in the most secret recesses of the earth; he who is skilled in attack flashes forth from the topmost heights of heaven. Thus on the one hand we have the ability to protect ourselves; on the other, a victory that is complete.

8 To see victory only when it is within the ken of the common herd is not the acme of excellence.

9 Neither is it the acme of excellence if you fight and conquer and the whole Empire says: 'Well done!'

10 To lift an autumn leaf is no sign of great strength; to see the sun and moon is no sign of sharp sight; to hear the noise of thunder is no sign of a quick ear.

11 What the ancients called a clever fighter is one who not only wins, but excels in winning with ease.

12 Hence his victories bring him neither reputation for wisdom nor credit for courage.

13   He wins his battles by making no mistakes. Making no mistakes is what establishes the certainty of victory, for it means conquering an enemy that is already defeated.

14   Hence the skilful fighter puts himself into a position which makes defeat impossible, and does not miss the moment for defeating the enemy.

15   Thus it is that in war the victorious strategist only seeks battle after the victory has been won, whereas he who is destined to defeat first fights and afterwards looks for victory.

16   The consummate leader cultivates the Moral Law, and strictly adheres to method and discipline; thus it is in his power to control success.

17   In respect of military method, we have, firstly, Measurement; secondly, Estimation of quantity; thirdly, Calculation; fourthly, Balancing of chances; fifthly, Victory.

18   Measurement owes its existence to Earth; Estimation of quantity to Measurement; Calculation to Estimation of quantity; Balancing of chances to Calculation; and Victory to Balancing of chances.

19   A victorious army opposed to a routed one, is as a pound's weight placed in the scale against a single grain.

20   The onrush of a conquering force is like the bursting of pent-up waters into a chasm a thousand fathoms deep.

The Best Vision is Insight

Self-control, discipline and patience are key attributes for any leader, and this is what Sun Tzu's chapter on Tactical Dispositions is concerned with. The message to today's business leader is that the capacity to bide one's time and exercise restraint is crucial. Until you have possession of all the necessary information you cannot confidently gain an insight into the competition's likely next move, nor know the right moment at which to strike. Just as impulsiveness that leads to wading into action too early exposes an army's vulnerabilities for the enemy to exploit, so it is in modern commerce. Keep your cards close to your chest and don't gift the competition any unnecessary advantages.

The message is perfectly encapsulated in the chapter's first passage, which states that, "The good fighters of old first put themselves beyond the possibility of defeat, and then waited for an opportunity of defeating the enemy.'

Of critical importance here is understanding that the victory is in the planning. Battles for commercial supremacy are won and lost not in the marketplace, but in the strategizing and the timing. Get those right, and once you hit the market you are well positioned to succeed, or to react swiftly and successfully to the unexpected, thanks to the contingencies you will have built in. This brings with it invaluable time and cost savings.

The Exceptional Leader

The exceptional leader will have a penetrating discernment and an unusually keen vision that sets them apart from their peers and contemporaries and transcends that which can be taught and learned through experience. Sun Tzu is making the point that, yes, preparation and planning is key, but with all things being equal, sometimes you need that intangible extra insight that sets apart the born from the cultivated leader. As he says, 'One may know how to conquer without being able to do it.'

Family businesses are a good example of how an instinct for leadership and a feel for business cannot be passed on regardless of whose genes have been bequeathed or which venerable business school has been attended. Ideally, succession planning should ignore the familial bonds and look only to the premium leadership candidate from either within or without that can best consolidate gains and grow the company.

Gucci is a prime and tragic example. The fashion brand started by Guccio Gucci at the start of the 20th century evolved under his talented and ambitious son, Aldo, whose keen eye and steady hand became a byword for high-end Italian style. However, with all sorts of ill-equipped and mostly talentless descendants and relations increasingly coveting a piece of the action, a united strategy made way for fierce in-fighting among egos, that concluded with Aldo's nephew, Maurizio, being killed in 1995 by a hitman hired by his ex-wife. Normal order was only restored once the Gucci family were ousted from the firm that still bears their name.

Switch It Up

The leader must know what it is they want to achieve to be able to effectively set an agenda and communicate it to those who will be responsible for carrying it out. This agenda may be defensive or offensive depending on

the prevailing economic winds. This ability to switch it up at any given time to reflect changing conditions is an important leadership quality, while shifting between offence and defence – or appearing to – is an especially useful tactic to bring to bear in negotiations to draw out the true intentions of those around the table and so secure the best outcomes. All-conquering and peculiarly oxymoronic mainstream punk magazine *Vice* was built on a series of bluffs around distribution and backing that didn't exist until – thanks to the tactic – it did.

Sun Tzu reminds us, 'Security against defeat implies defensive tactics; ability to defeat the enemy means taking the offensive.'

The rapid retreat from globalization is a broad defensive tactic born out of ubiquitous geopolitical and existential concerns. Take your pick from pestilence, war, climate change, energy security, or a whole lot more besides. When the world is worried, administrations look inwards and go into survival mode. At such times, world trade liberalization takes a back seat, often to be usurped by protectionism and on- or near-shoring.

However, the thrust towards a more sustainable type of development that is coming to mark the 21st century – in contrast to the wholly untenable consumption that was the hallmark of its immediate predecessor – does not mean that commerce has suddenly become a dirty word. Going green has not sounded the death knell for competition, with today's more enlightened players which factor in people and planet still as focused on profit as ever companies were. This means that while they may be subject to regulations that compel them to act or operate in a certain way, when they deem the right time has come to go on the offensive, they will not hold back.

When he says, 'To see victory only when it is within the ken of the common herd is not the acme of excellence,' Sun Tzu reminds us that brilliance is the preserve of the few, not the many.

Effective leaders must possess an elevated ability to map a path through the chaos, playing out all manner of potential scenarios to ensure that

if 'x' happens the response will be 'y'. Such industriousness is sure to reduce the scope for failure and increase the chances of success. Success will appear to have been achieved easily to the untrained eye because the unflappable, wise and diligent leader made it look that way by doing their homework. Here then, we can conclude that the general's job description is to oversee success for the army, not the pursuit of personal glory, which does nothing to further the interests of the State.

And the same is true for today's business leader, who must distinguish between the voice of the ego and the actual situation for the greater good of the company. *The Art of War* is clear that renown and acclaim should not be the leader's motivation when it states that, 'neither is it the acme of excellence if you fight and conquer and the whole Empire says: "Well done!"'

Sun Tzu also reminds us in chapter four of the importance of the nature of the leader's call to action. Get the rallying cry right and all stakeholders will collect around it. This is an essential complement to the dispassionate method and discipline that need to be applied to keep the army or company running like a well-oiled machine. It helps bring the 'why' to the equation as well as the 'how', which serves to bind the company together, because staff, investors and customers alike will know what it stands for and where it is headed.

Eliminating Risk is in the Planning

The Art of War is very clear and precise on the sequence of military methods that should be deployed, describing, 'firstly, Measurement; secondly, Estimation of quantity; thirdly, Calculation; fourthly, Balancing of chances; fifthly, Victory.'

When applied to today's business landscape, we see that Sun Tzu is stressing the importance of intelligence and preparation in charting

a course for corporate success, whereby a broad assessment of opportunities and risks must first be taken by the leader and then added to layer by ever more enlightened layer.

These layers will include a comprehensive analysis of the market, of the company and of the competition – informed not by conjecture or fanciful notions, but by data-led facts. Consequently, the consummate leader will be able to identify in-house strengths to further channel and develop or pinpoint rivals' advantages to be wary of. And perhaps even more importantly, this thorough review will enable them to put their finger on shortcomings within the company that are holding it back, and – so long as they possess the requisite humility – to recognize and address their own personal weaknesses that may be clouding their judgement and leading to sub-optimal outcomes. When placed alongside an accumulation of knowledge about the chinks in their competitors' armour, they will come to possess a 360° view of all relevant forces prevailing upon the battlefield. In so doing, the company can be steered resolutely towards the achievement of its objectives.

A Culture of Winning

The profoundly positive impact of completing the mission, no matter how modest the scope of the ambition, should not be underestimated as a means by which to motivate and lift morale. Folk love to win. Success breeds success and it really is the case that people get into a winning habit. Similarly, if there's no culture of success prevailing at a company, then the willingness for employees to go the extra mile to achieve the goals they've been set is simply not there, since they have come to accept that 'getting by' is OK. This is what today's business leader can safely glean from *The Art of War* when Sun Tzu says, 'A victorious army opposed to a routed one, is as a pound's weight placed in the scale against a single grain.'

Consumers and investors want to be associated with winning too. A company that is gaining market share is making headlines and has momentum. It signifies the future, and business and backing are drawn to it. Conversely, a company that's dealing with slowing sales and a smaller slice of the pie than it was used to will have a difficult time framing that positively and risks haemorrhaging support unless it can turn the tide.

This usually requires a radical repackaging, or innovative new approach, but if the leader or general only knows one way of winning, it's going to be difficult for them to adapt to the new conditions.

Think of Blockbuster Video, the home video and video game rental company, which dominated proceedings in the 1990s. However, it refused to accept the new digital way of consuming movies until it was too late, with senior management going further and further down a rabbit hole of obsolete bricks and mortar stores. It appears they became addicted to losing, so puzzling was their decision-making in the face of overwhelming evidence that a different approach needed to be adopted.

And they had plenty of time too. The company was in an enviable and seemingly unassailable position of virtual monopoly, and even had the opportunity to future-proof the firm by buying Netflix in 2001 for the bargain basement price of $50 million. At worst, such low-risk opportunities would have allowed it to hedge its bets and keep a finger in both camps. But still they ploughed on with an obviously redundant business model and continued to misidentify the primary competition. This led to falling revenues and share price and stores closing en masse until the writing was on the wall and bankruptcy and corporate annihilation came knocking.

That's losing. But to illustrate the snowball impact of winning, let's look at the Elvis Presley brand. So different and exciting was this young man for a nation's youth frustrated by prolonged post-war cultural austerity, that Elvis quickly became its biggest star.

The more his records sold, the more radio play they received, and the more TV appearances he made. As the free publicity and promotion grew, so did the audience, with the result that sales went stratospheric, Hollywood came calling and the money continued to pour in.

The brand had quickly come to transcend the man and remains as iconic today several decades after his death as ever it was. As a never-ending cash cow for those that control and benefit from his estate, it's the stuff of dreams.

So, success begets success and it's that propulsion and momentum that is hard for the market to resist.

Sun Tzu certainly knew its value when seeking to make the breakthrough against a seemingly immovable enemy. As he writes, 'the onrush of a conquering force is like the bursting of pent-up waters into a chasm a thousand fathoms deep.'

CHAPTER FIVE

ENERGY

1 Sun Tzu said: The control of a large force is the same principle as the control of a few men: it is merely a question of dividing up their numbers.

2 Fighting with a large army under your command is nowise different from fighting with a small one: it is merely a question of instituting signs and signals.

3 To ensure that your whole host may withstand the brunt of the enemy's attack and remain unshaken – this is effected by manoeuvres direct and indirect.

4 That the impact of your army may be like a grindstone dashed against an egg – this is effected by the science of weak points and strong.

5 In all fighting, the direct method may be used for joining battle, but indirect methods will be needed in order to secure victory.

6 Indirect tactics, efficiently applied, are inexhaustible as Heaven and Earth, unending as the flow of rivers and streams; like the sun and moon, they end but to begin anew; like the four seasons, they pass away to return once more.

7 There are not more than five musical notes, yet the combinations of these five give rise to more melodies than can ever be heard.

8 There are not more than five primary colours (blue, yellow, red, white and black), yet in combination they produce more hues than can ever be seen.

9 There are not more than five cardinal tastes (sour, acrid, salt, sweet and bitter), yet combinations of them yield more flavours than can ever be tasted.

10 In battle, there are not more than two methods of attack – the direct and the indirect; yet these two in combination give rise to an endless series of manoeuvres.

11   The direct and the indirect lead on to each other in turn. It is like moving in a circle – you never come to an end. Who can exhaust the possibilities of their combination?

12   The onset of troops is like the rush of a torrent which will even roll stones along in its course.

13   The quality of decision is like the well-timed swoop of a falcon which enables it to strike and destroy its victim.

14   Therefore the good fighter will be terrible in his onset, and prompt in his decision.

15   Energy may be likened to the bending of a crossbow; decision, to the releasing of a trigger.

16   Amid the turmoil and tumult of battle, there may be seeming disorder and yet no real disorder at all; amid confusion and chaos, your array may be without head or tail, yet it will be proof against defeat.

17   Simulated disorder postulates perfect discipline; simulated fear postulates courage; simulated weakness postulates strength.

18   Hiding order beneath the cloak of disorder is simply a question of subdivision; concealing courage under a show of timidity presupposes a fund of latent energy; masking strength with weakness is to be effected by tactical dispositions.

19   Thus one who is skilful at keeping the enemy on the move maintains deceitful appearances, according to which the enemy will act. He sacrifices something, that the enemy may snatch at it.

20   By holding out baits, he keeps him on the march; then with a body of picked men he lies in wait for him.

21   The clever combatant looks to the effect of combined energy, and does not require too much from individuals. Hence his ability to pick out the right men and utilize combined energy.

22   When he utilizes combined energy, his fighting men become as it were like unto rolling logs or stones. For it is the nature of a log or stone to remain motionless on level ground, and to move when on a slope; if four-cornered, to come to a standstill, but if round-shaped, to go rolling down.

23   Thus the energy developed by good fighting men is as the momentum of a round stone rolled down a mountain thousands of feet in height. So much on the subject of energy.

'T Ain't What You Do, It's the Way That You Do It

For Sun Tzu, the ability to harness, regulate and direct an army's energy so that it's applied in the right amount, the right way, and in the right place is a key differentiator. It's not enough to have a powerful army that one throws into battle hoping sheer force of numbers will tell.

An army is a complex and nuanced machine made up of many moving parts that can be employed in an almost infinite number of different ways. Yes, the object is victory, or the avoidance of defeat, but what success looks like can vary, and given the factors at play are different every time the general is engaged in battle, it is up to them to collect together the perfect list of ingredients for the fray and combine them, as only a master blender can, to provide sweet resonance and impact in the field.

And so it is for the business leader, as they draw on the right resources for the matter at hand.

Want to reshape, remould, or repair the company image? Get brainstorming with your public relations team.

Decided you need to expand your product line? The R&D department may need a bigger slice of the budget.

Facing an unexpected legal challenge? It could be time to add to or establish an in-house legal team.

This isn't to say that in the above examples these are the only departments that would be tasked with delivering on the goal; rather, that their importance at that juncture may be elevated from the normal course of things. This could be expressed in a number of different ways, such as the time spent working directly with the senior leadership team, the level of executive authority temporarily wielded, or the costs allocated to the relevant function, be it a department, product, service, or programme.

Signs and Signals

In fact, it is essential the company's priorities are communicated from top to bottom; that they permeate and imbue the organization – whatever its size – all the way from the corridors of power to the front line, ensuring collective thinking around a common goal.

Sun Tzu describes it thus: 'Fighting with a large army under your command is nowise different from fighting with a small one: it is merely a question of instituting signs and signals.'

Strategy must be transformed into specific and well understood procedures, actions, timelines and responsibilities for it to be effectively implemented. This should help to enhance efficiency and regulatory compliance by ensuring uniformity of performance and quality. However, strategic or mission statement changes deemed beneficial to the business often necessitate operational changes – and these may need to be initiated at short notice during abnormal conditions or emergencies. If handled badly, these can be unsettling for those at the coal face. Clear communication is key.

And in an era where businesses are increasingly aware of environmental, social and governance (ESG) considerations, Sun Tzu's 'signs and signals' may also need to be communicated beyond the company walls – both up and down the chain to suppliers and contractors. A prime

example of this is the manner in which companies' greenhouse gas outputs are measured and assessed in the form of Scope 1, 2 and 3 emissions, which affords insights into reduction opportunities for corporates across the full value chain.

Corporate Guerrillas

In chapter five, Sun Tzu is concerned with the military general manoeuvring his armies in the appropriate fashion for the matter at hand. He advocates mixing it up, utilizing both the no-nonsense, slug-it-out direct approach, as well as the subtler, less obvious, indirect take on things to befuddle and stupefy the opposition. The business leader too must adopt both modi operandi to remain unpredictable and difficult to read by the competition. This means they can utilize less conventional resources at their disposal to take on or defend against a larger, more established rival.

In the UK, discount supermarket chain, Aldi found itself in hot water with venerable high street icon, Marks & Spencer – favourite of the middle aged and the middle class. This was due to the latter declaring the former's Cuthbert the Caterpillar chocolate roll cake as too close a copy of its original, and rather more expensive, Colin the Caterpillar and taking it to court for infringement of copyright.

While the case may have had merit, Aldi chose to gently mock and ridicule its more upmarket rival in the court of public opinion on its social media pages. The public loved it and while Aldi may have had to make a few tweaks to the product to make it compliant as part of an undisclosed out of court accord, its indirect approach to dealing with the challenge won the hearts of a lot of shoppers. This constituted a far more important victory in the greater scheme of things. Sun Tzu would have been proud.

Challenging market conditions marked by cost-of-living concerns – against which background this played out – always serve to broaden

the appeal of cheaper grocery stores. Marks & Spencer should have been both alert and sensitive to these prevailing conditions, looking to celebrate and communicate its own credentials instead of picking a fight with a competitor many of its customers may already have been toying with the idea of trying out, yet resisting out of brand loyalty and a belief that the more expensive retailer aligned more closely with their own identity and values. So, its clumsy direct action seemed not only humourless and self-defeating, but tone deaf and mean-spirited too. In true David-like fashion the perception was that Aldi had succeeded in hurling a seemingly innocuous Twitter stone at the UK retail Goliath, scoring a direct hit in the process.

The Master Blender

In passages 7 to 9, Sun Tzu uses analogies of musical notes, colours and tastes to communicate his meaning that it is how you put things together that distinguishes the journeyman from the master craftsman. The latter is able to draw on an infinite toolbox of options to forge the perfect combination of actions and manoeuvres needed to outwit the opposition and deliver success.

As rock music has evolved into an established art form since it burst on to the scene in the 1950s, so the accumulated body of work has grown and grown. While there are seemingly infinite arrangements of melodies, the combination of unconscious musical influences and the fact that rock music has standardized chord progressions, means that to some ears different songs can sound remarkably similar. For the artist that penned their track first, this can lead to simmering resentment if its influence does not receive the acknowledgement they believe it should be accorded, especially if the subsequent track goes on to make millions. Narcissistic, paranoid and jealous personalities are particularly

prone to skewed perspectives where court actions are undertaken in the misguided belief the original track was deliberately purloined.

In truth, as well as there being subtle, but important differences in arrangement, the more successful artist has leveraged all manner of circumstances, including the advantage their established fame and brand has given them. Success isn't just about having the finished product. It's what you do with that finished product, which is where things like timing the market and having a network of support come in. And while those engaged in deliberate plagiarism as a short cut to fame and fortune must be called out, usually the rationale for the challenge is spurious and in most cases found to be without merit.

It's akin to saying one's army *should* have won on the battlefield when, in fact, it didn't. It lost.

The better leader won, because they understood what it took to write a hit and that it takes teamwork to make a hit. It is why the vast majority of such cases including ones involving megastars such as Taylor Swift and Ed Sheeran are dismissed.

This isn't to say that some claims are not legitimate, and there have been some famous challenges – not least from Motown legend Marvin Gaye's estate, which successfully argued in court in 2015 that Robin Thicke and Pharrell Williams' megahit, 'Blurred Lines' owed much to Gaye's 1977 track 'Got to Give it Up'. The upshot was that the long-dead Marvin Gaye was afforded a posthumous song-writing credit which translated to several million dollars.

The publicity surrounding the challenges will likely see musicians become more guarded as to their influences or serve to stifle creative discussion regarding the style or feel of a particular song having been informed by a prior work. This will be born out of fear, that any loose talk will stir up thoughts of a bumper payday from estate representatives that hitherto would have been oblivious to the opportunities to cash in that such musical homages presented. As it relates to Sun Tzu, this caginess

constitutes indirect defence tactics from similarly indirect guerrilla assaults that can increasingly come from anywhere and at any time.

Good Old-Fashioned Onslaughts

Yet, in this chapter of *The Art of War*, it is also made clear that an army needs to be on its guard against – as well as make use of – direct tactics. The value of such tactics must not be forgotten, since they afford the opportunity to subject the enemy to a series of unrelenting onslaughts, the sheer volume of which can end up being difficult to resist.

For a business, such a wave of assaults on the marketplace can successfully result in the subjugation of the competition.

So, when Sun Tzu writes that, 'The onset of troops is like the rush of a torrent which will even roll stones along in its course,' we can take from this that releasing a series of ever better new products or refinements to a service to the market in quick succession has the capacity to blow the competition away. If a rival doesn't respond in a timely fashion, the traction and excitement being generated by its adversary can result in a swift loss of market share, catastrophic erosion of profits and a share price in freefall.

This type of irresistible momentum and traction is exemplified by Apple's iPhone. Originally launched in 2007, the hand-held smart device, which had been developed in utmost secrecy, wowed the market like nothing before it with its computer quality software interface combined with best-in-class hardware.

With unprecedented functionality and uber-cool design credentials supported by Apple's brand strength and the power of its marketing, the Steve Jobs-led company succeeded in bringing smartphones to the masses. And with a market quickly hooked, almost annual follow-up versions kept it hungry for more and better, each new model eagerly anticipated in the

belief it represented an improvement on its predecessor, and in the knowledge that ownership would bring with it guaranteed bragging rights.

What's more, the iPhone's highly loyal following of adherents were – and still are – prepared to ignore the hefty price tag, such that the series of rapid-fire releases ended up wiping unprepared competitors like Blackberry and Nokia off the face of the map, as they struggled and failed to find an answer – any answer – with which to respond. Like Sun Tzu says, 'The quality of decision is like the well-timed swoop of a falcon which enables it to strike and destroy its victim.'

The latter sections in *The Art of War*'s chapter on Energy serve to remind us that appearances can be deceiving. When he says, 'Amid the turmoil and tumult of battle, there may be seeming disorder and yet no real disorder at all,' Sun Tzu is keen to let the reader know it's OK if the enemy thinks chaos reigns supreme within the ranks, so long as the truth is otherwise.

And when applied to the corporate sphere, even if one's own workforce cannot glean the purpose of what they've been tasked to do or perceive how it fits as part of an overall strategic pattern, there are moments in business – especially at critical 'all hands to the pump' moments – when there either isn't the opportunity for the leader to communicate the 'why', or they see no value in risking leaks or generating dialogue by oversharing. These are moments when it is legitimate for the leader to invoke executive authority and to expect of their employees that they place their faith in them.

In some cases, the business leader will seek to make a deliberate show of confusion or even promote a false narrative, in the understanding this will filter back to the competition, which will make a wrong move based on incorrect assumptions. It is another tool at the wise leader's disposal. And why Sun Tzu remarks, 'Thus one who is skilful at keeping the enemy on the move maintains deceitful appearances, according to which the enemy will act.'

CHAPTER SIX

WEAK POINTS AND STRONG

1   Sun Tzu said: Whoever is first in the field and awaits the coming of the enemy, will be fresh for the fight; whoever is second in the field and has to hasten to battle will arrive exhausted.

2   Therefore the clever combatant imposes his will on the enemy, but does not allow the enemy's will to be imposed on him.

3   By holding out advantages to him, he can cause the enemy to approach of his own accord; or, by inflicting damage, he can make it impossible for the enemy to draw near.

4   If the enemy is taking his ease, he can harass him; if well supplied with food, he can starve him out; if quietly encamped, he can force him to move.

5   Appear at points which the enemy must hasten to defend; march swiftly to places where you are not expected.

6   An army may march great distances without distress, if it marches through country where the enemy is not.

7   You can be sure of succeeding in your attacks if you only attack places which are undefended. You can ensure the safety of your defence if you only hold positions that cannot be attacked.

8   Hence that general is skilful in attack whose opponent does not know what to defend; and he is skilful in defence whose opponent does not know what to attack.

9   O divine art of subtlety and secrecy! Through you we learn to be invisible, through you inaudible; and hence we can hold the enemy's fate in our hands.

10   You may advance and be absolutely irresistible, if you make for the enemy's weak points; you may retire and be safe from pursuit if your movements are more rapid than those of the enemy.

11   If we wish to fight, the enemy can be forced to an engagement even though he be sheltered behind a high rampart and a deep ditch. All we need do is attack some other place that he will be obliged to relieve.

12   If we do not wish to fight, we can prevent the enemy from engaging us even though the lines of our encampment be merely traced out on the ground. All we need do is to throw something odd and unaccountable in his way.

13   By discovering the enemy's dispositions and remaining invisible ourselves, we can keep our forces concentrated, while the enemy's must be divided.

14   We can form a single united body, while the enemy must split up into fractions. Hence there will be a whole pitted against separate parts of a whole, which means that we shall be many to the enemy's few.

15   And if we are able thus to attack an inferior force with a superior one, our opponents will be in dire straits.

16   The spot where we intend to fight must not be made known; for then the enemy will have to prepare against a possible attack at several different points; and his forces being thus distributed in many directions, the numbers we shall have to face at any given point will be proportionately few.

17   For should the enemy strengthen his van, he will weaken his rear; should he strengthen his rear, he will weaken his van; should he strengthen his left, he will weaken his right; should he strengthen his right, he will weaken his left. If he sends reinforcements everywhere, he will everywhere be weak.

18   Numerical weakness comes from having to prepare against possible attacks; numerical strength, from compelling our adversary to make these preparations against us.

19   Knowing the place and the time of the coming battle, we may concentrate from the greatest distances in order to fight.

20   But if neither time nor place be known, then the left wing will be impotent to succour the right, the right equally impotent to succour the left, the van unable to relieve the rear, or the rear to support the van. How much more so if the furthest portions of the army are anything under a hundred li apart, and even the nearest are separated by several li!

21   Though according to my estimate the soldiers of Yueh exceed our own in number, that shall advantage them nothing in the matter of victory. I say then that victory can be achieved.

22   Though the enemy be stronger in numbers, we may prevent him from fighting. Scheme so as to discover his plans and the likelihood of their success.

23 Rouse him, and learn the principle of his activity or inactivity. Force him to reveal himself, so as to find out his vulnerable spots.

24 Carefully compare the opposing army with your own, so that you may know where strength is superabundant and where it is deficient.

25 In making tactical dispositions, the highest pitch you can attain is to conceal them; conceal your dispositions, and you will be safe from the prying of the subtlest spies, from the machinations of the wisest brains.

26 How victory may be produced for them out of the enemy's own tactics – that is what the multitude cannot comprehend.

27 All men can see the tactics whereby I conquer, but what none can see is the strategy out of which victory is evolved.

28 Do not repeat the tactics which have gained you one victory, but let your methods be regulated by the infinite variety of circumstances.

29 Military tactics are like unto water; for water in its natural course runs away from high places and hastens downwards.

30 So in war, the way is to avoid what is strong and to strike at what is weak.

31 Water shapes its course according to the nature of the ground over which it flows; the soldier works out his victory in relation to the foe whom he is facing.

32 Therefore, just as water retains no constant shape, so in warfare there are no constant conditions.

33 He who can modify his tactics in relation to his opponent and thereby succeed in winning, may be called a heaven-born captain.

34 The five elements (water, fire, wood, metal, earth) are not always equally predominant; the four seasons make way for each other in turn. There are short days and long; the moon has its periods of waning and waxing.

Improvise, Adapt, Overcome

Conditions on the battlefield and in the marketplace are ever changing and the best leader is a man or woman for all occasions, prepared and able to cope with any contingency.

That said, while the wiliest can prevail even when the odds are stacked against them, and it can help to occupy the hustle mindset of the underdog and even brand accordingly, one would prefer not to be disadvantaged.

Sun Tzu kicks off chapter six by talking about just such matters when he explains that 'Whoever is first in the field and awaits the coming of the enemy, will be fresh for the fight.'

In the business world this means first mover advantage, for if a company can set the agenda and provide the benchmark product or service against which all others to follow will be judged, the competition will have its work cut out to unseat the original brand and wrestle market share.

However, it's not the be-all and end-all to be the first mover, for there also exists everything from second to last mover advantage, where new entrants can study the pioneer and other forerunners' work and methods to strike on gaps in the market and to identify innovations and improvements that will resonate.

The capacity to exploit such openings in the market represents a big win at little outlay. As Sun Tzu says, 'An army may march great distances without distress, if it marches through country where the enemy is not.'

Nonetheless, it's important to remember that with both technology and the market ever-evolving, advantage is impermanent and ebbs and flows.

Sometimes even the biggest armies and the biggest brands find themselves on the back foot, no matter how seemingly durable and profound their upper hand. Coca-Cola, for example, had always enjoyed the edge over its rival Pepsi since both arrived on the scene in the late 19th century. That is, until the 1980s when slick sponsorship tie-ins from Pepsi saw it eclipse its arch-rival.

Coca-Cola panicked and responded with New Coke, a departure from the original formula and flavour. Met with outcry from the market, Coca-Cola was forced to beat a hasty retreat. However, in a development that none save perhaps the most cynically minded could claim to have foreseen, the restoration of the classic recipe to the shelves saw folk flock back in their droves to a brand they now seemingly forgot they had formerly given up on. It won back for Coca-Cola advantage in the Cola wars, which it maintains to this day.

Work Smart, Not Hard

At this juncture, *The Art of War* is also concerned with the concept of working smart, not hard.

An army's blood, sweat and tears will be for naught if that army is not being deployed with a specific purpose in mind. Similarly, a lack of direction in business means a workforce and its paymasters may believe there to be a high level of industry at play, but if there's nothing to show for it, it amounts to a poor use of resources.

Sun Tzu makes clear to the reader that seeking out the path of least resistance to the promised land constitutes the optimum approach when he says, 'You can be sure of succeeding in your attacks if you only attack

places which are undefended. You can ensure the safety of your defence if you only hold positions that cannot be attacked.'

This also means hitting the enemy or the competition at its most vulnerable points. For example, if a rival company releases worse than expected results that leads to a spooked market and a share price in freefall, this could be the time to release to the world your company's good news, even if it's not that new, and simply old news repackaged. This could speak to the recruitment of a new expert on to the team, a technological breakthrough, a product enhancement, an enriched customer service offering; anything, in fact, that works to differentiate and associate your company with value added, progress and success.

The comparison will likely not go unnoticed – even if only acknowledged subconsciously by those targets you seek to court – and can serve to generate maximum impact and to reassure at the expense of a rival at a time when it is, conversely, perceived to be in trouble.

Equally, if your company has bad news it is obliged to convey, there is no need to shout it from the rooftops. It will come as no surprise to learn that Friday afternoon at the end of the working week, when focus is turning to thoughts of the weekend, is a favourite time to bury sorry tidings in what is known as a 'Friday news dump'. By the time Monday rolls around the news cycle will have moved on, media scrutiny will be elsewhere, and there will be less scope for the competition to make hay from one's misfortune. As Sun Tzu points out, 'He is skilful in defence whose opponent does not know what to attack.'

Draw Out the Competition

Those opponents that occupy a seemingly impregnable position are not beyond engaging. The trick is to draw them into territory where you can compete. Sun Tzu understands this, when he says, 'If we wish to fight,

the enemy can be forced to an engagement even though he be sheltered behind a high rampart and a deep ditch. All we need do is attack some other place that he will be obliged to relieve.'

This capacity to rebalance the odds so they are not to your detriment is essential in business too. Though a competitor's first mover advantage may appear to have afforded it a virtual monopoly, there will be chinks in its armour, such as having deliberately shut out the competition. For in the US, as in many other economies, there are robust anti-trust laws to protect competition and consumers, representing a route by which companies can seek to gain access to the market or see introduced a more level playing field. Thereafter, a new entrant can come in at a markedly lower price or with a more user-friendly product by way of differentiating.

Microsoft is one such example, which was ultimately forced to compete in respect of operating systems software following a long-drawn-out case at the turn of the millennium. The upshot was that computer makers would subsequently be able to legitimately instal non-Microsoft browser software to run with Microsoft's operating system software. This ultimately led to the demise of the anachronistic Internet Explorer and to Microsoft being soundly beaten in the browser wars. The Seattle IT titan had complacently neglected to focus on advancing its browser to ensure it remained fit for purpose in anticipation of potential future competition, and then found itself obliged to divert its attentions to defending the indefensible, leaving itself vulnerable to attack. Sun Tzu could not have written it better.

The old Chinese master also uses this chapter to remind the reader that forewarned is forearmed, whereby prior knowledge equates to tactical advantage. Of course, for today's business leader corporate or industrial espionage is illegal, whereby the acquisition and/or use of an organization's proprietary information equates to theft or fraud, but what we can take from Sun Tzu is that knowledge of what is or is likely to come brings with it the opportunity to plan and make ready.

'Knowing the place and the time of the coming battle, we may concentrate from the greatest distances in order to fight,' he says.

And so it was for those pharmaceutical companies biding their time until Pfizer's 20-year patent on its hugely successful breakthrough erectile dysfunction drug, Viagra expired in jurisdictional stages from 2012, thereby allowing rivals to introduce to the market their own generic versions of the drug.

All parties knew the place and time of this battle and could have no excuse for not being prepared. The net result was that although Viagra's dominant market share was unsurprisingly substantially eroded, with a range of cut-price alternatives being approved and released, thanks to extraordinarily strong brand recognition it remains the market leader to this day. What's more, knowing what lay in store, it adapted its business model and responded with its own cheaper generic version, so softening the blow.

Provocation is a legitimate way for a company to discover a competitor's thinking and intentions and to identify its weak points. Sun Tzu says, 'Rouse him, and learn the principle of his activity or inactivity. Force him to reveal himself, so as to find out his vulnerable spots.'

Public baiting through any number of media channels – whether explicit or implicit – can be designed to elicit a response from a riled party. However, far from succeeding in putting a thorny issue to bed, a reaction instead serves to draw more spotlight on to the matter at hand. This alerts the provocateur to the fact they have touched a nerve, thereby confirming a suspected vulnerability, which can now be exploited.

Oftentimes, a dignified silence à la the British royal family's 'never complain, never explain' approach is the best way forward, since it confirms nothing, starves any gossip of oxygen, and gives to the organization the air of being unrattled and having more important things to do than respond to playground taunts. Any response from the House of Windsor to a very public roasting from one of their own was conspicuous

by its absence following the publication of Prince Harry's autobiography, *Spare*, jam-packed as it was with sensational and potentially reputation-damaging claims.

A spirited rebuttal may feel fleetingly empowering, but unless legally obliged to provide one, it can end up appearing doubtful in its sincerity and generating a tit for tat without end. As Shakespeare says in *Hamlet*, 'The lady doth protest too much, methinks.'

Probe and Shield

The advantage yielded by knowing the states of affair within a rival organization is a theme Sun Tzu returns to time and again. However, in war, even today, while rules of sort exist, the normal rules certainly do not apply, and so we need to adapt *The Art of War*'s message to fit within the modern corporate parameters.

One timeless process advocated in the ancient text is that of comparison. Today's most adept business leaders are theoretically capable of dispassionately observing the competition and contrasting it with their own set up in order to make the necessary adjustments and improvements to compete effectively. Assuming they have the correct inherent disposition and the appropriate qualities of mind and character to include in this assessment an acknowledgement of a rival's superiority in certain areas as well as their own shortcomings, the organization they head up could stand to benefit immeasurably from such a voyage of discovery. As Sun Tzu puts it, 'Carefully compare the opposing army with your own, so that you may know where strength is superabundant and where it is deficient.'

At the same time, it is important for a company to shield from the competition as much as it can about its inner workings, strengths, weaknesses and wider strategic intent. It is written so in *The Art of War*,

whereby Sun Tzu remarks, 'In making tactical dispositions, the highest pitch you can attain is to conceal them; conceal your dispositions, and you will be safe from the prying of the subtlest spies, from the machinations of the wisest brains.'

This concealment requires a team one can trust, and one that's fortunes are bound to the cause. Ensuring alignment of values at the recruitment stage as well as performance incentives can assist in this regard. On the other hand, loose talk, leaking of plans or lobbying against one's own paymasters can cause great damage to corporate prospects because they serve to ruin the element of surprise, which is the best form of attack. If rivals are aware of a company's intentions, they can steal a march and potentially get in there first, or alternatively, prepare a counter move to initiate when the anticipated assault comes.

The leader must be all seeing and all knowing, but what they choose to divulge and to whom is up to them. Selective disclosure of information to different team members on a need-to-know basis can be an effective means of maintaining control and can also help to smoke out disloyalty, since it will be easy to trace back to the source of any treachery.

And it can be an especially potent tool if that information is deliberately inaccurate and imparted to someone suspected of agitating or of being untrustworthy, thanks to the added potential win of such disinformation being taken for truth by a competitor that has received it through covert channels. And if a rival's reliance on such intelligence adversely impacts its fortunes, one can't help thinking it got its just desserts.

Perhaps no better example to prove this point can be cited than the 2022 legal spat between Colleen Rooney, wife of England soccer playing legend and later Washington-based DC United manager, Wayne Rooney; and Rebekah Vardy, whose husband is former England international, Jamie Vardy.

The WAG (Wives And Girlfriends) drama played out in excruciating detail across the pages of the British tabloid press, and resulted in a High

Court ruling in favour of Mrs Rooney, who had planted a story via her Instagram account that only Mrs Vardy could see, since she suspected her of leaking stories to the press. When the fake story in question went public, despite Rebekah Vardy's protestations of innocence, it was clear who the culprit was, and the incensed Colleen Rooney took little time in letting the world know via Twitter.

And while Mrs Vardy sought to restore her reputation through the courts, the fact that the evidence against her was overwhelming meant she only succeeded in compounding her woes in what became known as the 'Wagatha Christie' case, after the famed detective novelist. The upshot was that Rebekah Vardy's carefully curated image became forever profoundly tarnished, while Colleen Rooney's fortitude in the face of injustice and her super sleuth credentials saw her relatable 'ordinary woman', 'family first' identity, and by extension the Rooney brand, strengthened.

Sun Tzu concludes the chapter by emphasizing that the capacity to adapt rather than relying exclusively on 'tried and tested' methods or steadfastly adhering to a fixed 'come what may' strategy is essential. He exhorts the reader to 'let methods be regulated by the infinite variety of circumstances', and it's true that the wisest leaders keep the competition guessing with a constant flow of innovations. 'Just as water retains no constant shape, so in warfare there are no constant conditions' encapsulates his thinking.

CHAPTER SEVEN

MANOEUVRING

1   Sun Tzu said: In war, the general receives his commands from the sovereign.

2   Having collected an army and concentrated his forces, he must blend and harmonize the different elements thereof before pitching his camp.

3   After that, comes tactical manoeuvring, than which there is nothing more difficult. The difficulty of tactical manoeuvring consists in turning the devious into the direct, and misfortune into gain.

4   Thus, to take a long and circuitous route, after enticing the enemy out of the way, and though starting after him, to contrive to reach the goal before him, shows knowledge of the artifice of deviation.

5   Manoeuvring with an army is advantageous; with an undisciplined multitude, most dangerous.

6   If you set a fully equipped army in march in order to snatch an advantage, the chances are that you will be too late. On the other hand, to detach a flying column for the purpose involves the sacrifice of its baggage and stores.

7   Thus, if you order your men to roll up their buffcoats, and make forced marches without halting day or night, covering double the usual distance at a stretch, doing a hundred li in order to wrest an advantage, the leaders of all your three divisions will fall into the hands of the enemy.

8   The stronger men will be in front, the jaded ones will fall behind, and on this plan only one-tenth of your army will reach its destination.

9   If you march fifty li in order to outmanoeuvre the enemy, you will lose the leader of your first division, and only half your force will reach the goal.

10   If you march thirty li with the same object, two-thirds of your army will arrive.

11   We may take it then that an army without its baggage-train is lost; without provisions it is lost; without bases of supply it is lost.

12 We cannot enter into alliances until we are acquainted with the designs of our neighbours.

13 We are not fit to lead an army on the march unless we are familiar with the face of the country – its mountains and forests, its pitfalls and precipices, its marshes and swamps.

14 We shall be unable to turn natural advantage to account unless we make use of local guides.

15 In war, practise dissimulation, and you will succeed.

16 Whether to concentrate or to divide your troops must be decided by circumstances.

17 Let your rapidity be that of the wind, your compactness be that of the forest.

18 In raiding and plundering be like fire, in immovability like a mountain.

19 Let your plans be dark and impenetrable as night, and when you move, fall like a thunderbolt.

20 When you plunder a countryside, let the spoil be divided amongst your men; when you capture new territory, cut it up into allotments for the benefit of the soldiery.

21   Ponder and deliberate before you make a move.

22   He will conquer who has learnt the artifice of deviation. Such is the art of manoeuvring.

23   The Book of Army Management says: On the field of battle, the spoken word does not carry far enough: hence the institution of gongs and drums. Nor can ordinary objects be seen clearly enough: hence the institution of banners and flags.

24   Gongs and drums, banners and flags, are means whereby the ears and eyes of the host may be focused on one particular point.

25   The host thus forming a single united body, it is impossible either for the brave to advance alone, or for the cowardly to retreat alone. This is the art of handling large masses of men.

26   In night-fighting, then, make much use of signalfires and drums, and in fighting by day, of flags and banners, as a means of influencing the ears and eyes of your army.

27   A whole army may be robbed of its spirit; a commander-in-chief may be robbed of his presence of mind.

28   Now a soldier's spirit is keenest in the morning; by noonday it has begun to flag; and in the evening, his mind is bent only on returning to camp.

29   A clever general, therefore, avoids an army when its spirit is keen, but attacks it when it is sluggish and inclined to return. This is the art of studying moods.

30   Disciplined and calm, to await the appearance of disorder and hubbub amongst the enemy: – this is the art of retaining self-possession.

31   To be near the goal while the enemy is still far from it, to wait at ease while the enemy is toiling and struggling, to be well-fed while the enemy is famished: – this is the art of husbanding one's strength.

32   To refrain from intercepting an enemy whose banners are in perfect order, to refrain from attacking an army drawn up in calm and confident array: – this is the art of studying circumstances.

33   It is a military axiom not to advance uphill against the enemy, nor to oppose him when he comes downhill.

34   Do not pursue an enemy who simulates flight; do not attack soldiers whose temper is keen.

35   Do not swallow bait offered by the enemy. Do not interfere with an army that is returning home.

36   When you surround an army, leave an outlet free. Do not press a desperate foe too hard.

37   Such is the art of warfare.

Measure Twice, Cut Once

Chapter seven of *The Art of War* reminds us to plan and prepare meticulously and comprehensively, so that nothing is left to chance when it comes to taking action.

The Right People

For the business leader, both successful formulation of strategy and its implementation hinge upon having a dependable and skilled team around you. This encompasses both senior management and the front-line workers upon whose shoulders a company's fortunes rest, since there is little value in a strategy that cannot be realized due to an incompetent, unwilling, unreliable, ill-briefed or mismatched workforce.

Placing the right people in the right roles is of paramount importance. For example, maverick personalities with something of the loose cannon about them are unlikely to make good managers, that must lead by example. The presence of a volatile, pushy temperament in the office sounds like the stuff of nightmares, but it's an uncomfortable truth that such characters often make incredible salespeople; their tenacity, persistence and sheer bloody-mindedness meaning they won't accept 'no' and aren't satisfied until the sale has been achieved and their commission secured. They can be argumentative, disrespectful, frequently late to

work, but with sales the lifeblood of most organizations, such is their value, many companies are prepared to overlook this and much more if they keep the money rolling in.

You wouldn't trust them to run the payroll, let alone lead the company, but you have faith in them to drive revenue, and therefore they are an essential cog in the machine. Sun Tzu describes it thus when he refers to the make-up of the troops under the general's command: 'Having collected an army and concentrated his forces, he must blend and harmonize the different elements thereof before pitching his camp.'

Having a team that is 'up for the fight' brings with it major advantages. Well-trained, disciplined and motivated staff at a permanent state of readiness are able to rapidly respond to any curveball a competitor may put a company's way. They are also willing to go the extra mile when opportunity presents itself to ensure maximum gains are made before the window closes.

The leader knows that such concerted efforts involving the use of a lot of resources – perhaps involving expensive overtime – are sometimes necessary to win new business, since one must speculate to accumulate. Yet they must also accept there may be losses in the short term, and potentially a higher-than-normal turnover of staff who may feel overworked and insufficiently rewarded. This is to be expected 'if you order your men to roll up their buffcoats, and make forced marches without halting day or night, covering double the usual distance at a stretch...to wrest an advantage.'

In such instances the buck stops with the leader when it comes to convincing stakeholders these are acceptable losses within the context of the wider objective.

You can't stand still and expect victory to land in your lap in business any more than on the battlefield. The best leaders know it, just like Sun Tzu knew it, as epitomized by his assertion that, 'manoeuvring with an army is advantageous'.

He also knew that only the strongest and ablest are prepared to accept sacrifice today since they can envision the rewards that come with victory tomorrow, while others will not last the distance. It is these same characters today's business leader needs in their team to drive the company forward at their command. Just as Sun Tzu says, 'the stronger men will be in front, the jaded ones will fall behind.'

While filling team members with ambition and zeal that inspires them to strive for excellence and push towards new heights they formerly did not believe reachable is a laudable approach, it is also important for the leader not to be naïve. Tasking those under their charge to undertake the unachievable by committing them to an unnecessarily uphill battle or to dangle the carrot of rewards that are unobtainable is self-defeating.

For example, just as Sun Tzu knew 'that an army without its baggage-train is lost; without provisions is lost; without bases of supply is lost', so too must today's captains of industry ensure their company is not overstretched or without adequate resources, be that labour, financial or material, to complete the matter at hand.

Second Sight

Similarly, companies that enter into strategic alliances with others to enhance competitiveness, bring in expertise, diversify, mitigate risk, benefit from a capital injection, or for any other number of reasons, must be sure of the end game. It is essential that both parties know what they are letting themselves in for, since the corporate landscape is littered with failed marriages where one side leaves a lot better off than the other.

Venture capital investors may seem like knights in shining armour, but know that they are as clinical as it gets, and in it for the money, and the money alone. As such, there had better be a plan in place for when they

exit the stage. Equally, when negotiating at the outset of a company's journey, a business owner must be prepared to walk away if the deal on the table sees them giving away too much for too little in return.

The heady aroma of an investment within reach that would serve to accelerate a firm's fortunes is, for many, irresistible, but if the fruits of that success will mostly benefit others, or if it means all executive authority and capacity to steer the company will have to be relinquished, it is less than pointless. The best deals – the only deals worth striking – have both parties smiling. It is true that 'we cannot enter into alliances until we are acquainted with the designs of our neighbours.'

Equally, a company would be unwise to make a new foray into the market without knowing its state, just like a general would not send an army on the march without a thorough understanding of the landscape and conditions ahead.

Blindly pushing forward with a 'cross that bridge when we come to it' mindset is asking for trouble.

Most parents seek to inculcate in their children a responsible 'planning and saving' attitude that creates the conditions for resilience in the face of inevitable adversities to come that a hand-to-mouth existence cannot hope to deliver. And it is the same approach the business leader must adopt with their child, the company, where short-term thinking that only factors in immediate dynamics must be substituted for profound consideration of what will be necessary or may happen in the future. *The Art of War* speaks to this when Sun Tzu remarks that, 'we are not fit to lead an army on the march unless we are familiar with the face of the country – its mountains and forests, its pitfalls and precipices, its marshes and swamps.'

Lost in Translation

It is especially important to get the lie of the land when launching into a new market, particularly one with wholly different mores and traditions. To do so effectively requires local knowledge.

This would have been useful in Northern Ireland in the 1990s when the cell phone provider Orange UK (now EE, following a joint venture with Deutsche Telekom's T-Mobile UK), promoted the service with its go-to slogan, 'The future's bright, the future's Orange'. Unfortunately, this did not translate at all well in a binary market divided by religion: the Catholics on one side, the Protestants on the other. Given the latter had strong historical and present-day associations with the colour orange, not only did the company's core message alienate half of its potential market, but risked causing real offence at the same time.

As a branding blunder, the cell phone provider's is hard to top, but that doesn't appear to have stopped others with a similar lack of understanding of local sensitivities from trying. Carmakers, in particular, seem to have a penchant for causing offence with names for new models often translating very badly. Mazda's 'Laputa' ('La Puta' being 'The Wh*re' in Spanish!) takes first prize.

Meanwhile, the boom in big companies offshoring call centres in the 2000s to cheaper locales brought with it major frustrations for the caller at the other end. On top of often poor connections and long waiting times, when the caller eventually did get through, a combination of difficult to follow accents for the untrained ear and excruciating efforts from the operator to engage in prescribed casual chat about a culture they knew very little about, resulted in record numbers of complaints and customers leaving for companies that offered home country support.

Many companies came to the conclusion that reshoring such services made more financial sense in the long run. And Sun Tzu would agree.

He makes it abundantly clear that, 'we shall be unable to turn natural advantage to account unless we make use of local guides.'

If the landscape changes, it's important to reconsider one's approach based on the new information available, rather than persisting with a failing policy. It sounds obvious, but there's plenty out there that neglect to keep up with the state of play and continue down a rabbit hole born of dated rationale. The diligent leader will keep checking, because as Sun Tzu says, 'whether to concentrate or to divide your troops must be decided by circumstances.'

Pitch Perfect

The Art of War also makes clear in this chapter how important it is for a leader to recognize the efforts of those in their employ and to reward achievement. A soldier that feels valued will fight harder, and so it is with employees. The trick is to share the spoils of success fairly, whether in the form of promotions, bonuses, time off, or some other recompense, since failure to do so will only breed resentment from those parties believing themselves to have been overlooked or unfairly slighted, which can morph into troublemaking. Sun Tzu puts it succinctly, as only he can, when he says, 'let the spoil be divided amongst your men; when you capture new territory, cut it up into allotments for the benefit of the soldiery.'

Being fair and just is of crucial importance, and so is clear communication. When there is a specific task to do, the leader must avoid ambiguous instructions that could be interpreted in multiple ways, otherwise they must take responsibility for any failures that ensue. They must impart their meaning and relay their directives with both authority and clarity to ensure their wishes are faithfully executed. And this is equally applicable in respect of the company's public voice, which must

be pitch perfect across all available channels to cut through the market noise to reach and resonate with the intended targets. It is just how Sun Tzu describes it: 'Gongs and drums, banners and flags, are means whereby the ears and eyes of the host may be focused on one particular point.'

Most humans like to belong and to be part of an identifiable team. They want to be led, and so the leader at the top can harness that mentality to shift even a vast organization in a new direction. As Sun Tzu puts it, 'The host thus forming a single united body, it is impossible either for the brave to advance alone, or for the cowardly to retreat alone. This is the art of handling large masses of men.'

The managers, meanwhile, can be afforded more autonomy since they've been deputized to implement the strategy and need the leader's trust and the necessary space within which to do so.

And a big part of driving forward the pack involves keeping it motivated and upbeat. Sun Tzu sees it as maintenance and awareness of an army's 'spirit', and it is a vital function; one that involves factoring in adequate downtime so that spirits don't flag. Should they do so, prospects for success on the battlefield will diminish, and likewise, productivity at work will suffer.

Famed polar explorer Sir Ernest Shackleton is one of history's great motivators. Facing a seemingly hopeless situation when his ship *Endurance* was crushed by ice in the Antarctic in 1917 and he and his men stranded in the most inhospitable location on Earth, against impossible odds he kept his men optimistic, occupied and focused. Not only this, but he headed up a treacherous rescue mission across 1,300 km (800 miles) of vicious ocean, returning to find not a single man lost. Every leader needs a little bit of Shackleton about them.

The explorer was such a good leader since he was able to remain cool in a crisis, to adapt to the circumstances at hand and to exercise caution until such time as an assessment of the options could be made, and the

optimum way forward struck upon. His leadership credentials literally saved lives, as would the best generals' – both in Sun Tzu's day, and still today.

And while the contemporary business leader may not have life or death resting on their judgements, it remains the case they must not just avoid outward displays of panic or stress that serve to unsettle and bring with them the risk of contagion, but truly occupy a state of self-possession. Because being composed and in control of one's feelings allows for incisive decision-making from leaders for the greater good of the stakeholders in whose best interests they act. Many leaders find that life coaches can help them more readily access such a state of calmness, if that is something that does not come naturally to them.

It's fine for the competition to be panicking, but the consummate business leader should understand there is nothing inconsistent between a state of serenity informing one's decisions and business success. Sun Tzu knew it to be so, which is why he says, 'Disciplined and calm, to await the appearance of disorder and hubbub amongst the enemy: – this is the art of retaining self-possession.'

The leader with a meticulously researched strategy accounting for all manner of interruptions or challenges is one that has no cause for panic and no need for imposter syndrome. Their diligence and conscientiousness will mean they can hold their nerve against the most testing of conditions and know the right moment to strike. Their steady hand on the tiller will emanate an authoritative air to reassure the rank and file, preventing subversive behaviour born of fear from taking hold – fears perhaps about the company's prospects or of their own job security – allowing them to keep the faith.

CHAPTER EIGHT

VARIATION IN TACTICS

九變

1   Sun Tzu said: In war, the general receives his commands from the sovereign, collects his army and concentrates his forces.

2   When in difficult country, do not encamp. In country where high roads intersect, join hands with your allies. Do not linger in dangerously isolated positions. In hemmed-in situations, you must resort to stratagem. In desperate positions, you must fight.

3   There are roads which must not be followed, armies which must not be attacked, towns which must not be besieged, positions which must not be contested, commands of the sovereign which must not be obeyed.

4   The general who thoroughly understands the advantages that accompany variation of tactics knows how to handle his troops.

5   The general who does not understand these, may be well acquainted with the configuration of the country, yet he will not be able to turn his knowledge to practical account.

6   So, the student of war who is unversed in the art of war of varying his plans, even though he be acquainted with the Five Advantages [see page 13, Chapter One – Laying Plans], will fail to make the best use of his men.

7   Hence in the wise leader's plans, considerations of advantage and of disadvantage will be blended together.

8   If our expectation of advantage be tempered in this way, we may succeed in accomplishing the essential part of our schemes.

9   If, on the other hand, in the midst of difficulties we are always ready to seize an advantage, we may extricate ourselves from misfortune.

10   Reduce the hostile chiefs by inflicting damage on them; and make trouble for them, and keep them constantly engaged; hold out specious allurements, and make them rush to any given point.

11   The art of war teaches us to rely not on the likelihood of the enemy's not coming, but on our own readiness to receive him; not on the chance of his not attacking, but rather on the fact that we have made our position unassailable.

12   There are five dangerous faults which may affect a general:

(1) recklessness, which leads to destruction;

(2) cowardice, which leads to capture;

(3) a hasty temper, which can be provoked by insults;

(4) a delicacy of honour which is sensitive to shame;

(5) over-solicitude for his men, which exposes him to worry and trouble.

13   These are the five besetting sins of a general, ruinous to the conduct of war.

14   When an army is overthrown and its leader slain, the cause will surely be found among these five dangerous faults. Let them be a subject of meditation.

Knowledge is Not Power

It's all very well knowing what the goal is or what the received wisdom is in any given situation, and how to mix it up so as not to be predictable, but if a leader is rendered inert by analysis paralysis, or hesitant – incapable even – of putting their understanding of the rules, their grasp of the brief, or their well-researched theories into practice, then the knowledge they have accrued is meaningless. And if any lingering self-doubt means the actions they do end up taking are half-hearted and over-cautious, the outcome will likely not be good.

A leader must be decisive and fully committed. This is different to being headstrong. Rather, it means they have faith in their own abilities and know that to influence events talk must turn to action. At the same time, they will be alert to the fact that circumstances may change, necessitating a change of tack.

The brief may have come from someone above to whom the leader is answerable, be that a controlling shareholder, the tax authority, or increasingly, public sentiment, given the shift towards greater economic democracy. Knowing the objective is a good starting point from which to formulate the path to action. Chapter eight of *The Art of War* kicks off with a crisp, succinct assertion of this reality when it states that 'In war, the general receives his commands from the sovereign, collects his army and concentrates his forces.'

No Time for Inertia

It is essential for a leader to recognize and acknowledge when the odds are stacked against them and to act accordingly, confiding in and discussing with trusted close confidantes to formulate the right move. If it's a particularly challenging market, for example, then belts will need to be tightened. This can often mean cutting the workforce, since labour is for most businesses far and away the biggest cost.

With a company's payroll burden encompassing so much more than gross salary, to include taxes, pension and healthcare contributions, bonuses, paid time off and other expenses and perks, acting swiftly and decisively to reduce the load – even factoring in severance costs – can act to steady a ship in choppy waters. Conversely, doing nothing in hope things will pick up is an extremely risky strategy. Sun Tzu knew that when an army found itself in a sticky situation with danger all about, the worst thing to do was to stay put. Which is why he writes, 'When in difficult country, do not encamp...Do not linger in dangerously isolated positions.'

The tech sector's famed progressive credentials that purport to strain at the leash for ever better conditions, policies and methods is, yet, no more immune to the impact of market realities than any other section of the economy. Therefore, in times of falling advertising revenue and mounting costs fuelled by high inflation, even the tech giants determine the optimum response to adversity is to cut jobs and freeze hiring. Google, Meta, Amazon and Microsoft cumulatively laid off tens of thousands from their workforce in late 2022/early 2023.

Healthy Competition

Perhaps the overwhelming message of *The Art of War* is that there are alternatives to fighting. Sometimes a foe represents such a threat they

must be challenged, other times they are best left alone due to their superiority which brings to engagement the prospect of annihilation. However, for today's corporate chiefs, it's worth remembering that competition underpins a healthy free market economy and is considered a thing of sanctity. Monopolies, therefore, are discouraged via anti-trust legislation, given that they act to stifle choice for the consumer, leaving them open to exploitation.

With this in mind, there exists today a measure of protection, in contrast to the lack of oversight in Sun Tzu's time. Consequently, for bigger high-profile businesses, scope for an appeal to a higher force exists when all other options to meaningfully compete with an overbearing rival have expired. Google again, (or rather its parent company, Alphabet), with a market capitalization of over $1.2 trillion, has repeatedly found itself in hot water and been subject to eye-watering fines for violation of competition laws. In this case it is the US Department of Justice itself that has led the charge.

That said, unless the government starts to deem one's firm a societal menace or even an existential threat – and most business leaders will never face such a situation – the anti-trust landscape does tend to be systemically biased in favour of big business. Because of this, smaller business owners will sometimes be obliged to accept defeat and retreat or move to more promising ground – perhaps a new untapped location or by introducing new product lines – if they intend to prosper, since digging in against a rival that is able to deploy unmatchable economies of scale is just plain daft.

Just sometimes, it works the other way around. Local government – often in response to impassioned community pleas – may restrict multinationals' access to a location famed for its independent retailers, and in such cases, it is the bigger army that must retreat or admit defeat in that battle and turn its attentions elsewhere.

In short, for all armies, all businesses, 'There are roads which must

not be followed, armies which must not be attacked, towns which must not be besieged, positions which must not be contested, commands of the sovereign which must not be obeyed.'

Knowledge is the Starting Point, Not the End Game

Knowledge is essential – both knowledge of the external realities involving the market terrain and the competition; and of one's in-house competencies, but in and of itself will not deliver success. Rather, it should be viewed as the source material governing tactics. To translate that knowledge at any given time into meaningful impact is what's important. It is why Sun Tzu asserts that, 'The general who does not understand [the advantages that come with variation of tactics], may be well acquainted with the configuration of the country, yet he will not be able to turn his knowledge to practical account.'

Different conditions demand different approaches. An understanding of what these approaches look like can be learned to a degree, but must also be hard won through experience, to wit: a savvy leader will need to experience failure and the bitter taste of defeat to fine-tune their corporate response to stimuli.

While a sound leader will be focused on generating traction and forward momentum for the concern they represent, they will want at the same time to ensure the competition is on the back foot and remains there. When a company is preoccupied with firefighting and in survival mode it is unable to divert resources to mount an operation to knock off course a rival's ambitions. This effectively gifts to the other party a freer run at the market, and if it's a two-horse race, a veritable blank canvas upon which to paint and give form to its strategy.

Sun Tzu asks that those seeking advantage, 'Reduce the hostile chiefs

by inflicting damage on them; and make trouble for them, and keep them constantly engaged.'

These days, companies that can master the art of social media have to hand hugely influential conduits from which to potentially control the narrative and keep the competition from getting on the front foot. Insinuating, implying, inferring i.e. permissible mud-throwing at a rival means some is likely to stick, and if done well so that it speaks to an authentic pain point for consumers, it will see the competition having to tie up time and resources in PR management. This often starts with its failure to acknowledge or even its blind denial of an issue, followed by prolonged attempts to wrestle back advantage as the under-fire firm wards off panic both within and without by attempting to present as united, empathetic, authentic and transparent.

Knowing the pain points and working behind the scenes to address them is even more important than knowing and channelling one's strengths, because the competition will know them too and will seek to take advantage. It is the leader's job to anticipate this and have in place the appropriate response.

Pride Before a Fall

For political leaders, whose opponents are constantly looking for any excuse to discredit them, they can safely assume any skeletons in their closet will be revealed in time, given that the holders of their secrets are as predisposed towards confession as anyone else. In which case, they'd better have the right response prepared, or even strategically determine that the best approach is to get in there first before the opposition does, especially if a story is about to go public, so that they can control the narrative.

Alternatively, what some leaders do is say nothing and do nothing in response, brushing it off as a storm in a teacup if pressed. However, unless you're a king or queen installed in perpetuity, this strategy will eventually hit a dead end, as former UK Prime Minister, Boris Johnson discovered in 2022.

Mounting allegations regarding the British leader's personal conduct and of those under his watch were dismissed by him with a jocularity that had served him well in the past but was now deemed increasingly inappropriate. A general indignation at an apparent sense of entitlement rapidly grew and came to reach a critical mass, whereby he lost the support of his once adoring public and party members and was driven out of office. The moral of the story here is that, as 'The art of war teaches us...rely not on the likelihood of the enemy's not coming, but on our own readiness to receive him.'

CHAPTER NINE

THE ARMY ON THE MARCH

行軍

1   Sun Tzu said: We come now to the question of encamping the army, and observing signs of the enemy. Pass quickly over mountains, and keep in the neighbourhood of valleys.

2   Camp in high places, facing the sun. Do not climb heights in order to fight. So much for mountain warfare.

3   After crossing a river, you should get far away from it.

4   When an invading force crosses a river in its onward march, do not advance to meet it in mid-stream. It will be best to let half the army get across, and then deliver your attack.

5 If you are anxious to fight, you should not go to meet the invader near a river which he has to cross.

6 Moor your craft higher up than the enemy, and facing the sun. Do not move up-stream to meet the enemy. So much for river warfare.

7 In crossing salt-marshes, your sole concern should be to get over them quickly, without any delay.

8 If forced to fight in a salt-marsh, you should have water and grass near you, and get your back to a clump of trees. So much for operations in salt-marshes.

9 In dry, level country, take up an easily accessible position with rising ground to your right and on your rear, so that the danger may be in front, and safety lie behind. So much for campaigning in flat country.

10 These are the four useful branches of military knowledge which enabled the Yellow Emperor to vanquish four other sovereigns.

11 All armies prefer high ground to low and sunny places to dark.

12 If you are careful of your men, and camp on hard ground, the army will be free from disease of every kind, and this will spell victory.

13 When you come to a hill or a bank, occupy the sunny side, with the slope on your right rear. Thus you will at once act for the benefit of your soldiers and utilize the natural advantages of the ground.

14 When, in consequence of heavy rains up-country, a river which you wish to ford is swollen and flecked with foam, you must wait until it subsides.

15 Country in which there are precipitous cliffs with torrents running between, deep natural hollows, confined places, tangled thickets, quagmires and crevasses, should be left with all possible speed and not approached.

16 While we keep away from such places, we should get the enemy to approach them; while we face them, we should let the enemy have them on his rear.

17 If in the neighbourhood of your camp there should be any hilly country, ponds surrounded by aquatic grass, hollow basins filled with reeds, or woods with thick undergrowth, they must be carefully routed out and searched; for these are places where men in ambush or insidious spies are likely to be lurking.

18 When the enemy is close at hand and remains quiet, he is relying on the natural strength of his position.

19 When he keeps aloof and tries to provoke a battle, he is anxious for the other side to advance.

20 If his place of encampment is easy of access, he is tendering a bait.

21 Movement amongst the trees of a forest shows that the enemy is advancing. The appearance of a number of screens in the midst of thick grass means that the enemy wants to make us suspicious.

22 The rising of birds in their flight is the sign of an ambuscade. Startled beasts indicate that a sudden attack is coming.

23 When there is dust rising in a high column, it is the sign of chariots advancing; when the dust is low, but spread over a wide area, it betokens the approach of infantry. When it branches out in different directions, it shows that parties have been sent to collect firewood. A few clouds of dust moving to and fro signify that the army is encamping.

24 Humble words and increased preparations are signs that the enemy is about to advance. Violent language and driving forward as if to the attack are signs that he will retreat.

25 When the light chariots come out first and take up a position on the wings, it is a sign that the enemy is forming for battle.

26   Peace proposals unaccompanied by a sworn covenant indicate a plot.

27   When there is much running about and the soldiers fall into rank, it means that the critical moment has come.

28   When some are seen advancing and some retreating, it is a lure.

29   When the soldiers stand leaning on their spears, they are faint from want of food.

30   If those who are sent to draw water begin by drinking themselves, the army is suffering from thirst.

31   If the enemy sees an advantage to be gained and makes no effort to secure it, the soldiers are exhausted.

32   If birds gather on any spot, it is unoccupied. Clamour by night betokens nervousness.

33   If there is disturbance in the camp, the general's authority is weak. If the banners and flags are shifted about, sedition is afoot. If the officers are angry, it means that the men are weary.

34 When an army feeds its horses with grain and kills its cattle for food, and when the men do not hang their cooking-pots over the camp-fires, showing that they will not return to their tents, you may know that they are determined to fight to the death.

35 The sight of men whispering together in small knots or speaking in subdued tones points to disaffection amongst the rank and file.

36 Too frequent rewards signify that the enemy is at the end of his resources; too many punishments betray a condition of dire distress.

37 To begin by bluster, but afterwards to take fright at the enemy's numbers, shows a supreme lack of intelligence.

38 When envoys are sent with compliments in their mouths, it is a sign that the enemy wishes for a truce.

39 If the enemy's troops march up angrily and remain facing ours for a long time without either joining battle or taking themselves off again, the situation is one that demands great vigilance and circumspection.

40 If our troops are no more in number than the enemy, that is amply sufficient; it only means that no direct attack can be made. What we can do is simply to concentrate all our

available strength, keep a close watch on the enemy, and obtain reinforcements.

41 He who exercises no forethought but makes light of his opponents is sure to be captured by them.

42 If soldiers are punished before they have grown attached to you, they will not prove submissive; and, unless submissive, they will be practically useless. If, when the soldiers have become attached to you, punishments are not enforced, they will still be useless.

43 Therefore soldiers must be treated in the first instance with humanity, but kept under control by means of iron discipline. This is a certain road to victory.

44 If in training soldiers commands are habitually enforced, the army will be well-disciplined; if not, its discipline will be bad.

45 If a general shows confidence in his men but always insists on his orders being obeyed, the gain will be mutual.

Pay Attention to the Signs

Any leader worth their salt should have a vision of where they want their company to get to, and one which they can share to inspire, excite and motivate. However, that which distinguishes the effective leader is the ability to shepherd, guide and direct the organization towards that destination.

While always being mindful of the objective is key, unless a leader is focused on the journey and making sound decisions based on the evidence in front of them, the goal will inexorably recede ever further into the distance. Stakeholders will forgive stumbles and detours necessitated by market dynamics at any given time, but expect measurable and palpable progress towards the grail, and of a leader that they are able to interpret the landscape as necessary to make the right choices.

In chapter nine, *The Art of War* is concerned with all sorts of landscapes and makes very clear that when things are, objectively and unalterably, a certain way, at that juncture, there are certainties and truths that regulate how one should proceed.

While Sun Tzu was concerned with what to do when confronted by, variously, mountains, rivers, salt marshes and open plains, today's corporate masters with something to sell must understand that a buyer's market, for example, will demand a different approach to one where customers are beating a path to its door. Recognizing what's out there will allow a company to navigate accordingly and ultimately reach and

successfully engage its intended targets more swiftly and at reduced cost.

Distance Lends Disadvantage

It is the case that distance often lends disadvantage if one wants to be aware of the state of the market and what competitors are doing. Strategy needs to be tested, with general theories formulated in the workplace needing to be checked and piloted to determine whether they have real world application, be it via focus groups, outreach programmes, loss leader products, free trials or other such initiatives. If there is existing customer goodwill towards a company, best use should be made of this to maximize alignment and support, cement consumer loyalty and to reinforce the brand. When Sun Tzu talks of mooring upstream of a target, he is speaking about just such natural advantage.

If a culture of furtiveness and taking covert untrodden paths becomes the norm at a company, it can serve to isolate it from its customers, so much so it loses an understanding of what those customers want and need and fails to connect ideas and practices to them. The company in question may also lose sight of what the competition is doing, so focused is the firm on its own hidden agenda, which can become increasingly uninformed by the wider landscape. Sun Tzu warns against seeking refuge in, travelling through or settling in high places for too long since the apparent oversight it gives of the market is an illusion.

There are Few Short Cuts to Success

These passages can also be interpreted as a warning to today's business leaders that the peak performance demanded of a team by challenging

conditions can only be sustained for so long, and that as well as being taxing for employees, lingering in such high-pressure environments can also work to quickly drain financial resources. If such a path must be taken, let there be a clear and well understood purpose behind it, and best efforts made to ensure more nurturing and nourishing working conditions are restored as soon as possible. As Sun Tzu remarks, 'After crossing a river, you should get far away from it.'

The business leader, just like the general, has no time to dally, since the market is restless and never sleeps, so a period of high demands that saps a team's energy and necessitates time out to recuperate could be a less productive way to proceed in the long run despite the quick-win advantages a period of intense working appeared to promise at the outset. This is especially true of a company with only a small team wearing many hats at its disposal, since there is not access to other human resources to pick up the slack. And if talent cannot be brought to bear, it is left exposed. The wise leader knows a company's employees are its greatest asset and must be looked after to ensure long-term gain.

Paths that afford advantage or easy passage are certain to lift morale among the corporate troops, which is why Sun Tzu talks of sunny, hard ground being not only to soldiers' benefit, but also that which meets their preference. Conversely, if one tarries in an inhospitable location jam-packed with obstacles to overcome, this is sure to promote a gloomy defeatist outlook born from prolonged hardship. This can quickly spread to become a contagion within the ranks which is bound to impact productivity.

The takeaway here is that embracing danger is foolhardy and risks inviting catastrophe. For today's business bigwigs, it makes sense to wait for a moment of lower risk opportunity, even if it comes with scope for less immediate reward. Better this than suffering huge losses or risk being wiped off the face of the map for ignoring clear portents of doom. It is why Sun Tzu says, 'When, in consequence of heavy rains up-country, a river which you wish to ford is swollen and flecked with foam, you must wait until it subsides.'

Obstacles to Progress Guaranteed

The Art of War dedicates much space to detailing various obstacles and their capacity to restrict free movement and passage. For any business there are impediments denoting real and present danger and therefore potential harm to its prospects.

The sudden imposition of tariffs is one such example. The USA and China are locked in an ongoing battle for economic supremacy and – depending on the prevailing political winds of the day – are prone to slapping duties on all manner of products and services with very little advance warning in a tit for tat that can quickly escalate to throttle trade across all sorts of sectors.

For companies with business models predicated on foreign sales or with product lines reliant on foreign imports, such ebbing and flowing geopolitical power plays over which they have no control have the unwelcome side effect of severely damaging their interests. The US automotive and agriculture sectors are particularly exposed to such measures.

In an age of increasing deglobalization that harks back to isolationist eras of the past, it pays then for companies not only to keep their ear to the ground for rumblings of what's to come, but also to futureproof by way of domestic supply chain diversification both up and downstream. In this way, they will secure advantage over competitors facing the same set of dynamics. For Sun Tzu, 'Country in which there are precipitous cliffs with torrents running between, deep natural hollows, confined places, tangled thickets, quagmires and crevasses should be left with all possible speed and not approached.'

Forever Alert

As well as a capacity to spy opportunity when others don't, exemplary leadership also involves being constantly mindful of dangers all about. To get on in business means being proactive, but this inevitably brings with it some measure of exposure to risk. And while only a fool would willingly court danger, sometimes the only way to success lies through unpredictable territory. It pays then to be watchful in such circumstances, and to know that others' values about what is acceptable in business may be markedly different from one's own.

For example, attending trade shows is, for many companies, an un-beatable way to network, to strike new business and strengthen existing relationships. Because being able to press the flesh forges a much more potent connection than any number of Zoom meetings can ever hope to achieve. However, the competition is likely to have the same belief structure, in which case you will be in close proximity within a confined space.

It would be counter-productive for a company to approach conver-sations with potential new leads at its stand from a starting place of suspicion or thinly veiled hostility because it feared this was the competition operating incognito. At the same time, however, it would be wise not to overshare, and certainly not give over the blueprints for a soon to launch top secret new product!

Equally, when it comes to rivals making off with a firm's most valued staff or its best customers, it is up to the leader to guard closely any such assets that are integral to the success of the company and reward them appropriately. This could be in the form of thoughtful working conditions, a long contract, unmatched customer service, competitive prices, or any other number of measures that will keep them loyal. And that's because one thing is certain: if a company puts itself out there – which surely it must – other companies will try to take for themselves the

good bits. For his part, Sun Tzu describes many hiding spots, pointing out that, 'these are places where men in ambush or insidious spies are likely to be lurking.'

The Evidence is Out There

Accurately determining what the competition's next move is must be made up of more than a leader's best guesstimate. While these days, there are all sorts of prohibitions forbidding the type of illicit information gathering that would allow one to easily arrive at that point, one can nonetheless infer from evidence and reasoning what the 'enemy' is up to.

A competitor's public face can yield a certain amount of useful information. For example, if it is less communicative and forthcoming than usual on its social media platforms, or if it has held off on the advertising, marketing or PR, this means something may be brewing. Lying low could indicate the rival is making itself ready for a major launch or campaign, or on the other side of the spectrum, that it is in financial trouble and has been compelled to rein in all discretionary expenditure.

Determining whether a competitor is on the ropes or never been in ruder health can likely be established through conversations with suppliers; by looking at the recruitment arena to see whether the company in question is hiring or firing; or by analysing its quarterly reports.

Ask oneself: Has a new person recently been installed at the top that is no doubt going to want to put their own stamp on things and make an impact? It also doesn't hurt to take a look at staff's personal posts in the public domain to see if they betray anything about the company they work for, since, while they should know better, away from work, folk can be less guarded and may let things slip regarding disaffection within the ranks they occupy.

Also, look for signs within one's own company to surmise what the other lot is doing: Have sales or enquiries been dropping off? Have customers or staff been jumping ship or become less engaged?

Being able to self-pose questions without ego to strike on an accurate assessment of one's own performance and that of the firm is an important yet oft overlooked leadership quality. If after this, the leader can strike on no clear root cause of a dip in company fortunes, while this could be the consequence of a depressed economy, it could also be that the other company is just now doing things better, and thus, there is an urgent need to adapt and innovate to compete.

And so it was in Sun Tzu's day in the military realm, where he details a wide variety of indicators that can be interpreted to allow for timely action. In one such vivid passage he explains, 'The rising of birds in their flight is the sign of an ambuscade. Startled beasts indicate that a sudden attack is coming.'

In trading too, it's all about paying attention to the signs. And while insider dealing sees stocks illegally traded by those in possession of material confidential information yet to be made public and is considered to afford unfair advantage, the best traders will legitimately use a mixture of technical and fundamental analysis to read the signs to determine future price movements, and thus what constitutes good opportunity. This sees them crunching the numbers as well as looking at wider economic and financial factors.

Beware of Overtures

While cordial and mutually respectful relations with competitors should be the leader's aim for the company, and there may, on occasion, even be scope for collaborations, one mustn't lose sight of the fact that business is a competition. Firms target the same audience with comparable

products or services to secure more sales, gain a bigger slice of the market and generate greater revenues than their rivals. Against such a backdrop, it should come as no surprise that wily tactics will be deployed to get ahead.

How a company behaves vis-à-vis competitors says a lot about it. Naïvety at leadership level here will likely be replicated across all sorts of company endeavours to the ultimate detriment of the firm, and points to a management populated by inexperienced people-pleasing folk. Even the highest echelons of the corporate sphere have their fair share of snake oil salesmen, and in fact, those ignoble renegades that have made it to the top will be very accomplished charlatans. It is essential then to know how to spot one so as not to succumb to their siren-like charms that seek only to gain from others' misfortune.

These days, a gentleman's agreement or a handshake is ultimately not worth the paper it's written on and putting into motion plans based upon such uncontracted commitments would be a mistake, since these verbal bonds are difficult to prove in the event one party goes back on its word. Sun Tzu goes further, asserting unequivocally that, 'Peace proposals unaccompanied by a sworn covenant indicate a plot.'

How to Bind a Team to the Cause

The order of the day for leaders here is to be firm but fair, to appear approachable and communicative, yet nobody's fool, such that no interlocutor could be in any doubt as to that leader's tireless dedication to prioritizing the interests of the company and all its stakeholders. Nor, under any illusion the leader will do anything save take decisive action to shut out or go after any interests that would seek to undermine or sabotage the company's mission.

This extends to one's own team, where it's wise to opt for the carrot

first, before wielding the stick, though ensuring staff know the stick is in the toolbox to be used as and when necessary.

For new leaders, especially those drafted in from outside, it is essential to first incentivize and win over a potentially – and understandably – wary set of faces before contemplating tougher approaches to pushing through an agenda. Once the team is bound to the cause and to the leader spearheading it, individuals will be less resistant to a firmer management style, since there will be fewer co-workers prepared to join in with a show of solidarity. Sun Tzu notes in this regard that, 'Soldiers must be treated in the first instance with humanity, but kept under control by means of iron discipline. This is a certain road to victory.'

It is important to note here, that once the team's allegiance has been secured, it is sensible to move to a less familiar relationship with one's employees, for if they believe a leader to be on the same level, they will also instinctively believe them to be malleable and exploitable. Consequently, the leader's instructions are less likely to be carried out effectively, or even at all. At that point, authority is irretrievably lost, and with it the ability to lead. In this respect, a willingness to resist micromanaging, and rather to empower those under their charge, is the best approach a leader can take to ensuring employees do not come to resent the executive authority which resides in them. For Sun Tzu, the benefits for both sides of such an approach were clear: 'If a general shows confidence in his men but always insists on his orders being obeyed, the gain will be mutual.'

CHAPTER TEN

TERRAIN

地形

1   Sun Tzu said: We may distinguish six kinds of terrain, to wit:

(1) Accessible ground;

(2) entangling ground;

(3) temporizing ground;

(4) narrow passes;

(5) precipitous heights;

(6) positions at a great distance from the enemy.

2   Ground which can be freely traversed by both sides is called accessible.

3   With regard to ground of this nature, be before the enemy in occupying the raised and sunny spots, and carefully guard your line of supplies. Then you will be able to fight with advantage.

4   Ground which can be abandoned but is hard to reoccupy is called entangling.

5   From a position of this sort, if the enemy is unprepared, you may sally forth and defeat him. But if the enemy is prepared for your coming, and you fail to defeat him, then, return being impossible, disaster will ensue.

6   When the position is such that neither side will gain by making the first move, it is called temporizing ground.

7   In a position of this sort, even though the enemy should offer us an attractive bait, it will be advisable not to stir forth, but rather to retreat, thus enticing the enemy in his turn; then, when part of his army has come out, we may deliver our attack with advantage.

8   With regard to narrow passes, if you can occupy them first, let them be strongly garrisoned and await the advent of the enemy.

9   Should the army forestall you in occupying a pass, do not go after him if the pass is fully garrisoned, but only if it is weakly garrisoned.

10 With regard to precipitous heights, if you are beforehand with your adversary, you should occupy the raised and sunny spots, and there wait for him to come up.

11 If the enemy has occupied them before you, do not follow him, but retreat and try to entice him away.

12 If you are situated at a great distance from the enemy, and the strength of the two armies is equal, it is not easy to provoke a battle, and fighting will be to your disadvantage.

13 These six are the principles connected with Earth. The general who has attained a responsible post must be careful to study them.

14 Now an army is exposed to six calamities, not arising from natural causes, but from faults for which the general is responsible. These are:

(1) Flight;

(2) insubordination;

(3) collapse;

(4) ruin;

(5) disorganization;

(6) rout.

15   Other conditions being equal, if one force is hurled against another ten times its size, the result will be the flight of the former.

16   When the common soldiers are too strong and their officers too weak, the result is insubordination. When the officers are too strong and the common soldiers too weak, the result is collapse.

17   When the higher officers are angry and insubordinate, and on meeting the enemy give battle on their own account from a feeling of resentment, before the commander-in-chief can tell whether or not he is in a position to fight, the result is ruin.

18   When the general is weak and without authority; when his orders are not clear and distinct; when there are no fixed duties assigned to officers and men, and the ranks are formed in a slovenly haphazard manner, the result is utter disorganization.

19   When a general, unable to estimate the enemy's strength, allows an inferior force to engage a larger one, or hurls a weak detachment against a powerful one, and neglects to place picked soldiers in the front rank, the result must be a rout.

20   These are six ways of courting defeat, which must be carefully noted by the general who has attained a responsible post.

21   The natural formation of the country is the soldier's best ally; but a power of estimating the adversary, of controlling the forces of victory, and of shrewdly calculating difficulties, dangers and distances, constitutes the test of a great general.

22   He who knows these things, and in fighting puts his knowledge into practice, will win his battles. He who knows them not, nor practises them, will surely be defeated.

23   If fighting is sure to result in victory, then you must fight, even though the ruler forbid it; if fighting will not result in victory, then you must not fight even at the ruler's bidding.

24   The general who advances without coveting fame and retreats without fearing disgrace, whose only thought is to protect his country and do good service for his sovereign, is the jewel of the kingdom.

25   Regard your soldiers as your children, and they will follow you into the deepest valleys; look upon them as your own beloved sons, and they will stand by you even unto death.

26   If, however, you are indulgent, but unable to make your authority felt; kind-hearted, but unable to enforce your

commands; and incapable, moreover, of quelling disorder: then your soldiers must be likened to spoilt children; they are useless for any practical purpose.

27   If we know that our own men are in a condition to attack, but are unaware that the enemy is not open to attack, we have gone only halfway towards victory.

28   If we know that the enemy is open to attack, but are unaware that our own men are not in a condition to attack, we have gone only halfway towards victory.

29   If we know that the enemy is open to attack, and also know our men are in a condition to attack, but are unaware that the nature of the ground makes fighting impracticable, we have still gone only halfway towards victory.

30   Hence the experienced soldier, once in motion, is never bewildered; once he has broken camp, he is never at a loss.

31   Hence the saying: If you know the enemy and know yourself, your victory will not stand in doubt; if you know Heaven and know Earth, you may make your victory complete.

When the Ego Dies, the Soul Awakens

The early passages of *The Art of War*'s chapter on Terrain are given over to discussion of all types of ground and the different means by which a general should respond. Similarly, for today's business generals, the market terrain will vary; sometimes benevolent, sometimes hostile, and companies must take this into account when determining whether, when or how to act.

If the landscape is wholly or partially obscured – especially if a competitor already holds sway or market advantage in niche areas – it pays to hold fire until such time the contours of the land are revealed, since blindly deploying resources significantly impacts prospects for a return on investment. For Sun Tzu, such terrain is not 'accessible ground', but rather, any number of: 'entangling ground, narrow passes, precipitous heights, or positions at a great distance from the enemy'.

The Lie of the Land

The general, or today's business leader 'who has attained a responsible post must be careful to study them', since each requires different thinking and methodology.

Changes to the regulatory environment, for example, can boost or harm a company's chances. If potential adjustments or developments to current regulations are being argued out in the corridors of power, but a finely balanced debate means it is, as yet, unclear what the outcome will be, it makes sense to wait before committing to a strategy that is predicated on the rules being a certain way.

In a host of countries, sugar taxes designed to prevent obesity and safeguard public health have either already been introduced or soon will be. This has obliged food and drink manufacturers active in these jurisdictions to revisit their business models.

In the US, however, there has been more resistance, with soda taxes only levied in certain localized instances. Yet, with research suggesting there has been a sustained impact on sugar intake in those regions, American beverage companies in particular would be wise to factor in the possibility of this levy being scaled up and applied across the nation.

Across the pond, the General Data Protection Regulation, better known by its acronym 'GDPR' is a European Union (EU) privacy law requiring of companies that they take responsibility for keeping personal data held safe. Penalties for non-compliance can be severe, encompassing hefty fines, reputational damage, loss of productivity and even imprisonment. Just ask tech giants Amazon, Meta and Google, each of which have been penalized to the tune of hundreds of millions of dollars since the regulation came into force.

In a further twist to events, with the United Kingdom having exited the EU since GDPR became law, this allowed it the independence to keep the framework under review, meaning companies operating in the UK must be alert to further changes on the horizon to ensure continued compliance.

The introduction of new compliance requirements – whether it's to protect consumers, employees, or the resilience of the industry a company sits within – are not necessarily going to destroy a firm. However, there

will be costs involved and decisions will need to be taken about whether these can be absorbed, whether cuts must be made to certain budgets, or if the hit can be passed on to customers. And all the while, a company must be mindful of how other firms in the same position are likely to respond in order to remain competitive.

Firms that invest in creating an effective regulatory change management framework will not only be in a better position to anticipate potentially critical rule changes, but are also set up to prepare in advance a range of strategic responses to be implemented calmly and at speed. This leaves them well placed to secure market advantage in any revised market landscape just when others may be in a state of disarray, desperately trying to adapt to the new reality. So, while a company will rightfully be reluctant to make a move in advance of knowing the full facts, there is no value in procrastinating when the mist clears, for the terrain has ceased to become 'temporizing'. This is how Sun Tzu describes ground, 'when the position is such that neither side will gain by making the first move.'

Following the severe global economic crisis that unfolded across 2007 and 2008, which had its origins in an inadequately regulated financial services sector, the pendulum swung sharply the other way, ushering in an era of rigid oversight as part of attempts to avoid a repeat crash.

This state-sponsored superintendence and onus on financial services organizations to put their houses in order brought to firms in the space onerous and costly new capital requirements and reporting obligations, leading to squeezed margins. Those institutions that attempted to carry on as normal had a rude awakening, with stiff penalties and loss of bonuses acting as a stick to force through changes in culture and behaviour. Such circumstances can become difficult to escape from with Sun Tzu describing this terrain as 'entangling ground' that is 'hard to reoccupy'. However, if a company can exercise authority and assert control in this challenging environment, 'From a position of this sort, if the enemy is unprepared, you may sally forth and defeat him.'

Meanwhile, the allure of enhanced reputation with stakeholders that was clearly coming to those acting more responsibly and embracing change in an increasingly ethically-conscious investment environment, served to catalyse the process.

The Destructive Leader

A mediocre, egotistical or downright incompetent leader can destroy a company. While it's no small ask, during their tenure they must be all seeing, all knowing, yet at the same time, not have the organization so dependent on them it cannot survive their departure. This means ensuring there are robust processes in place for the seamless transfer of power to guarantee a smooth handover.

It is essential for an organization's long-term health that the mantle of authority bestowed upon a leader does not get fused with that person's personality, and that its prospects are not irreparably damaged should that individual no longer remain in post. Rather, the executive dominion vested in them should seamlessly be able to be assumed and channelled by a new figure.

The company must be bigger than any one individual, for as they say, there's no 'I' in team.

The best strategies will have the interests of the company, not the captain at their heart and will rely on the entire corporate machine working in concert to be successfully implemented, where all relevant persons are as disinclined towards unilateralism as hopefully the person at the top is.

Success depends on communication and all stratas of the organization buying into the strategy so they can pull in the same direction. If this collective mindset is not present, 'When the higher officers are angry and insubordinate, and on meeting the enemy give battle on their own account from a feeling of resentment, before the

commander-in-chief can tell whether or not he is in a position to fight, the result is ruin.'

This is not to say the leader does not have a huge say in how things will pan out. Sun Tzu says, 'An army is exposed to six calamities, not arising from natural causes, but from faults for which the general is responsible.'

In the corporate sphere, a narcissistic leader that lets their ego get the better of them can bring down a firm with poor decision-making or unethical and autocratic ways. These characters are more common than one would imagine, and the dysfunctional example they set can quickly permeate the whole organization. If things look like they're going to go – or are going – south under their watch, it is essential they can be removed.

The six calamities *The Art of War* refers to – namely: flight, insubordination, collapse, ruin, disorganization and rout – can always be traced back to the leader's door. Deficient leaders can make the wrong call on when to strike the market; attempt to out-compete too strong a rival; recruit poorly to key roles; fail to unite a disparate team in pursuit of a common goal, gather insufficient intelligence, or make any number of errors of judgement that can contribute directly or indirectly to damaging or destroying a company's prospects. Sun Tzu's thinking is encapsulated in his statement that, 'When the general is weak and without authority; when his orders are not clear and distinct; when there are no fixed duties assigned to officers and men, and the ranks are formed in a slovenly haphazard manner, the result is utter disorganization.'

True humility that sees any natural human proclivity towards vices like pride, greed and envy substituted in favour of community thinking will see leaders exercise the kind of authority that inspires and irresistibly draws a team to them. Employees can see that this is decision-making informed not by glory-seeking, but by a desire to act in the best interests of the organization, and which is born of objective analysis. It is why Sun Tzu says that, 'The general who advances without coveting fame and retreats

without fearing disgrace, whose only thought is to protect his country and do good service for his sovereign, is the jewel of the kingdom.'

The Art of War reminds the reader that just as a general must view the soldiers under their command through the same lens they would their own children, so too must the business leader treat their employees with similar selflessness to command the type of loyalty and respect a child has for its parent. These children – both soldiers and employees – can be wayward at times, and must suffer the parent's correction when at fault, since this is part of the caregiving they must be in receipt of to make guided progress. And just like a child, they will be more inclined to give respect to those providing boundaries and less likely to rebel. It is just as Sun Tzu says; 'If, however, you are indulgent, but unable to make your authority felt; kind-hearted, but unable to enforce your commands; and incapable, moreover, of quelling disorder: then your soldiers must be likened to spoilt children; they are useless for any practical purpose.'

CHAPTER ELEVEN

THE NINE SITUATIONS

九地

1 Sun Tzu said: The art of war recognizes nine varieties of ground:

(1) Dispersive ground;

(2) facile ground;

(3) contentious ground;

(4) open ground;

(5) ground of intersecting highways;

(6) serious ground;

(7) difficult ground;

(8) hemmed-in ground;

(9) desperate ground.

2   When a chieftain is fighting in his own territory, it is dispersive ground.

3   When he has penetrated into hostile territory, but to no great distance, it is facile ground.

4   Ground the possession of which imports great advantage to either side, is contentious ground.

5   Ground on which each side has liberty of movement is open ground.

6   Ground which forms the key to three contiguous states, so that he who occupies it first has most of the Empire at his command, is a ground of intersecting highways.

7   When an army has penetrated into the heart of a hostile country, leaving a number of fortified cities in its rear, it is serious ground.

8   Mountain forests, rugged steeps, marshes and fens – all country that is hard to traverse: this is difficult ground.

9　Ground which is reached through narrow gorges, and from which we can only retire by tortuous paths, so that a small number of the enemy would suffice to crush a large body of our men: this is hemmed-in ground.

10　Ground on which we can only be saved from destruction by fighting without delay, is desperate ground.

11　On dispersive ground, therefore, fight not. On facile ground, halt not. On contentious ground, attack not.

12　On open ground, do not try to block the enemy's way. On the ground of intersecting highways, join hands with your allies.

13　On serious ground, gather in plunder. In difficult ground, keep steadily on the march.

14　On hemmed-in ground, resort to stratagem. On desperate ground, fight.

15　Those who were called skilful leaders of old knew how to drive a wedge between the enemy's front and rear; to prevent co-operation between his large and small divisions; to hinder the good troops from rescuing the bad, the officers from rallying their men.

16　When the enemy's men were united, they managed to keep them in disorder.

17   When it was to their advantage, they made a forward move; when otherwise, they stopped still.

18   If asked how to cope with a great host of the enemy in orderly array and on the point of marching to the attack, I should say: 'Begin by seizing something which your opponent holds dear; then he will be amenable to your will.'

19   Rapidity is the essence of war: take advantage of the enemy's unreadiness, make your way by unexpected routes, and attack unguarded spots.

20   The following are the principles to be observed by an invading force: The further you penetrate into a country, the greater will be the solidarity of your troops, and thus the defenders will not prevail against you.

21   Make forays in fertile country in order to supply your army with food.

22   Carefully study the well-being of your men, and do not overtax them. Concentrate your energy and hoard your strength. Keep your army continually on the move, and devise unfathomable plans.

23   Throw your soldiers into positions whence there is no escape, and they will prefer death to flight. If they will face death, there

is nothing they may not achieve. Officers and men alike will put forth their uttermost strength.

24 Soldiers when in desperate straits lose the sense of fear. If there is no place of refuge, they will stand firm. If they are in hostile country, they will show a stubborn front. If there is no help for it, they will fight hard.

25 Thus, without waiting to be marshalled, the soldiers will be constantly on the qui vive; without waiting to be asked, they will do your will; without restrictions, they will be faithful; without giving orders, they can be trusted.

26 Prohibit the taking of omens, and do away with superstitious doubts. Then, until death itself comes, no calamity need be feared.

27 If our soldiers are not overburdened with money, it is not because they have a distaste for riches; if their lives are not unduly long, it is not because they are disinclined to longevity.

28 On the day they are ordered out to battle, your soldiers may weep, those sitting up bedewing their garments, and those lying down letting the tears run down their cheeks. But let them once be brought to bay, and they will display the courage of a Chu or a Kuei.

29 The skilful tactician may be likened to the shuai-jan. Now the shuai-jan is a snake that is found in the Ch'ang mountains. Strike at its head, and you will be attacked by its tail; strike at its tail, and you will be attacked by its head; strike at its middle, and you will be attacked by head and tail both.

30 Asked if an army can be made to imitate the shuai-jan, I should answer, 'Yes'. For the men of Wu and the men of Yueh are enemies; yet if they are crossing a river in the same boat and are caught by a storm, they will come to each other's assistance just as the left hand helps the right.

31 Hence it is not enough to put one's trust in the tethering of horses, and the burying of chariot wheels in the ground.

32 The principle on which to manage an army is to set up one standard of courage which all must reach.

33 How to make the best of both strong and weak, that is a question involving the proper use of ground.

34 Thus the skilful general conducts his army just as though he were leading a single man, willy-nilly, by the hand.

35 It is the business of a general to be quiet and thus ensure secrecy; upright and just, and thus maintain order.

36   He must be able to mystify his officers and men by false reports and appearances, and thus keep them in total ignorance.

37   By altering his arrangements and changing his plans, he keeps the enemy without definite knowledge. By shifting his camp and taking circuitous routes, he prevents the enemy from anticipating his purpose.

38   At the critical moment, the leader of an army acts like one who has climbed up a height and then kicks away the ladder behind him. He carries his men deep into hostile territory before he shows his hand.

39   He burns his boats and breaks his cooking-pots; like a shepherd driving a flock of sheep, he drives his men this way and that, and nothing knows whither he is going.

40   To muster his host and bring it into danger: – this may be termed the business of the general.

41   The different measures suited to the nine varieties of ground; the expediency of aggressive or defensive tactics; and the fundamental laws of human nature: these are things that must most certainly be studied.

42   When invading hostile territory, the general principle is that penetrating deeply brings cohesion; penetrating but a short way means dispersion.

43   When you leave your own country behind, and take your army across neighbourhood territory, you find yourself on critical ground. When there are means of communication on all four sides, the ground is one of intersecting highways.

44   When you penetrate deeply into a country, it is serious ground. When you penetrate but a little way, it is facile ground.

45   When you have the enemy's strongholds in your rear, and narrow passes in front, it is hemmed-in ground. When there is no place of refuge at all, it is desperate ground.

46   Therefore, on dispersive ground, I would inspire my men with unity of purpose. On facile ground, I would see that there is close connection between all parts of my army.

47   On contentious ground, I would hurry up my rear.

48   On open ground, I would keep a vigilant eye on my defences. On ground of intersecting highways, I would consolidate my alliances.

49 On serious ground, I would try to ensure a continuous stream of supplies. On difficult ground, I would keep pushing on along the road.

50 On hemmed-in ground, I would block any way of retreat. On desperate ground, I would proclaim to my soldiers the hopelessness of saving their lives.

51 For it is the soldier's disposition to offer an obstinate resistance when surrounded, to fight hard when he cannot help himself, and to obey promptly when he has fallen into danger.

52 We cannot enter into alliance with neighbouring princes until we are acquainted with their designs. We are not fit to lead an army on the march unless we are familiar with the face of the country – its mountains and forests, its pitfalls and precipices, its marshes and swamps. We shall be unable to turn natural advantages to account unless we make use of local guides.

53 To be ignorant of any one of the following four or five principles does not befit a warlike prince.

54 When a warlike prince attacks a powerful state, his generalship shows itself in preventing the concentration of the enemy's forces. He overawes his opponents, and their allies are prevented from joining against him.

55 Hence he does not strive to ally himself with all and sundry, nor does he foster the power of other states. He carries out his own secret designs, keeping his antagonists in awe. Thus he is able to capture their cities and overthrow their kingdoms.

56 Bestow rewards without regard to rule, issue orders without regard to previous arrangements; and you will be able to handle a whole army as though you had to do with but a single man.

57 Confront your soldiers with the deed itself; never let them know your design. When the outlook is bright, bring it before their eyes; but tell them nothing when the situation is gloomy.

58 Place your army in deadly peril, and it will survive; plunge it into desperate straits, and it will come off in safety.

59 For it is precisely when a force has fallen into harm's way that it is capable of striking a blow for victory.

60 Success in warfare is gained by carefully accommodating ourselves to the enemy's purpose.

61 By persistently hanging on the enemy's flank, we shall succeed in the long run in killing the commander-in-chief.

62 This is called the ability to accomplish a thing by sheer cunning.

63 On the day that you take up your command, block the frontier passes, destroy the official tallies, and stop the passage of all emissaries.

64 Be stern in the council-chamber, so that you may control the situation.

65 If the enemy leaves a door open, you must rush in.

66 Forestall your opponent by seizing what he holds dear, and subtly contrive to time his arrival on the ground.

67 Walk in the path defined by rule, and accommodate yourself to the enemy until you can fight a decisive battle.

68 At first, then, exhibit the coyness of a maiden, until the enemy gives you an opening; afterwards emulate the rapidity of a running hare, and it will be too late for the enemy to oppose you.

How to Play
Follow the Leader

The Art of War returns to the subject of different types of ground in chapter eleven. It is a key theme for Sun Tzu. He is telling us it is madness to make life unnecessarily difficult by taking the most challenging routes. Such a path is self-defeating and to the detriment of the horde. Therefore, he wants chieftains to know what conditions combine to make up difficult, serious, contentious, desperate and other types of ground, and how they should act accordingly in each case to either ensure advantage or ward off disadvantage, all the while preserving as many resources as possible.

And masochists don't win in business any more than they do on the battlefield. The pyramid hierarchy that exists beneath the leader is collectively motivated by a need for the leader to wisely and empathetically drive forward change and deliver results with informed decision-making. The soldier or employee is prepared – happy even – to relinquish personal autonomy in return for someone else (the leader) acting as the bulwark from life's demands. If the leader consistently makes – and is seen to make – the right calls and creates the right enabling conditions for the provision of the regular pay packet that allows for the worker to be a functioning part of society, they will have a vested interest in following them.

A Life of Service

The complete leader will know when to strike and when to hold back, dependent upon the prevailing conditions and landscape. Adopting a mindset that accepts the authority vested in them has been delegated and entrusted to them by numerous stakeholders, including those ostensibly less senior, is a fast track to becoming a better leader.

The leader is in service no less than the front-line operatives and is there to represent them and act in their best interests. Such pure thinking reflected in their actions and behaviour will see the leader become a magnet, effortlessly drawing in those they seek to court.

Splintering the Opposition

When engaging the opposition, a timeless approach no less relevant today than it was when *The Art of War* was written is to divide and conquer, affording the opportunity to sow discord among competitors' ranks and so redirect ire and other hostile behaviours back on to the source of the bother.

It can be an especially potent device when looking to repel encroachment on to one's natural territory. Sun Tzu understands as much when he writes that, 'Those who were called skilful leaders of old knew how to drive a wedge between the enemy's front and rear; to prevent co-operation between his large and small divisions; to hinder the good troops from rescuing the bad, the officers from rallying their men.'

This enables a smaller firm to take on a bigger one by splitting the market the latter may have a monopoly over into more manageable and less coherent groups. For example, this can be achieved via thought leadership pieces, blogs and other posts and campaigns that seek to

influence the narrative of the industry in question and indirectly tap into pain points and unmet objectives – be they financial, value or ambition-based – from the competition's customer base.

Targeting critical elements of a rival's operations – for example, by muscling in on limited critical supplies that each side covets, via a needling advertising campaign, or through slashing prices on key lines – may see the targeted company pulling in different directions to meet the threat. Here, silo mentalities start to become established and valuable information stops being shared between departments. Under such a scenario, certain personnel may conclude their needs and wants will be better served by jumping ship to a company with which they feel more aligned.

Internally, the leader must use more uplifting and positive approaches that seek to lead by example, rather than endeavour to sow infighting in the ranks below to preserve their own position. As well as running the risk of introducing a combative workplace culture that is hard to reverse, in-house divide and rule also speaks to insecurity unbecoming of a strong leader.

The need for co-ordinated team-wide responses is of crucial importance. In Sun Tzu's teachings, different business departments can be seen as 'the men of Wu and the men of Yueh', whom he describes as 'enemies'. In spite of this, he makes clear that, 'if they are crossing a river in the same boat and are caught by a storm, they will come to each other's assistance just as the left hand helps the right.'

Meanwhile, a willingness to publicly engage with one's own customers – especially those that leave negative feedback – will help to nip in the bud and mitigate the impact of any adverse publicity, as well as connecting one's offer with transparency and a spirit of listening.

How to Inspire Devotion

It is the case that crises can only be averted when the leader is in control and can rely on others to carry out their instructions. Sun Tzu knows that when backs are against the wall and to relent or succumb is to risk defeat or death, the soldier will be able to access and display new levels of dogged determination and fearlessness. Similarly, if those that work for a company are bound to the cause; are loyal to and trust in the leader, they will answer the call to arms and assiduously apply themselves to the calamity at hand.

'Soldiers when in desperate straits lose the sense of fear. If there is no place of refuge, they will stand firm. If they are in hostile country, they will show a stubborn front. If there is no help for it, they will fight hard.'

So says Sun Tzu. And by this he means all is not necessarily lost, even when the situation appears bleak, since existential crises can bring out the best in people, so long as the leader has been an even-handed caregiver. Care equally meted out and an ability to position staff in roles that play to their respective strengths breeds unanimity of purpose within an organization.

Meanwhile, those human assets that collect around a vision and meet the leader's stated expectations must be rewarded, for they collectively constitute the oracle from which insights are gleaned to both strike upon and to deliver on objectives with confidence.

And rewarding success acts to nourish the workforce and to bring to the team a sense of solidarity. This must be in place and able to be called upon if a company expects to ride out the bad times. Sun Tzu reminds us that one must 'Make forays in fertile country in order to supply your army with food.'

He also makes clear that the leader must, 'Carefully study the well-being of your men, and do not overtax them. Concentrate your energy and hoard your strength.'

Controlling the Flow of Information

Looking after one's troops or staff to ensure they remain loyal, devoted and committed also means not overburdening them with information they've no business knowing and that may serve to unsettle them. Critical plans such as those relating to a major upcoming offensive on the battlefield or the market, or outright bad news, likely only require sharing on a need-to-know basis. People are not so much disloyal as inherently confessional, so keeping news of what's to come or word on the gravity of a situation within a close-knit circle of trusted confidantes until the time is ripe, reduces the scope for leaks and panic. Sun Tzu notes that, 'It is the business of a general to be quiet and thus ensure secrecy; upright and just, and thus maintain order.'

Across the world, as the dust began to settle on the COVID-19 pandemic and there came the opportunity for reflection and analysis, governments were angrily rebuked by the people on whose behalf they were acting. This, for the manner in which they had managed the flow of information and for their respective rationales for taking action, as they sought to accurately interpret data to determine when and to what degree to impose lockdowns, what levels of financial support to provide, how to procure and distribute personal protective equipment (PPE) and vaccines, and much else besides, while all the time seeking to ward off national panic and maintain law and order.

The collective charge laid against them that they had withheld critical information neglected to acknowledge that the authorities in question were wholly unprepared for the scale and harsh realities of the challenges facing them; that they were seeking to balance the public's demand for transparency with the fact that they themselves were scrabbling for answers to strike upon the appropriate responses. The deeply unsettling effects of admitting this in real time would have made it difficult for the powers that be to maintain order and security, potentially leading to societal collapse.

The leader must expect to be relentlessly targeted since toppling them represents the prize scalp and would have the biggest adverse ripple effect. Whether it's rival firms or pretenders to the crown within the organization, the head honcho must accept as part of the territory that others will seek to attach to them a reputation for unethical behaviour, rule breaking or incompetency.

Awareness of this means the leader must endeavour to be whiter than white in their personal conduct and stay the right side of all the relevant rules and regulations, while remaining shrewd and discerning. It's a very fine balancing act, but leadership is akin to treading a tightrope, and to expect others to follow, one must lead by example.

For Sun Tzu, doing away with the leader is something he sees as a clear objective. 'By persistently hanging on the enemy's flank, we shall succeed in the long run in killing the commander-in-chief,' he says.

CHAPTER TWELVE

ATTACK BY FIRE

1   Sun Tzu said: There are five ways of attacking with fire. The first is to burn soldiers in their camp; the second is to burn stores; the third is to burn baggage trains; the fourth is to burn arsenals and magazines; the fifth is to hurl dropping fire amongst the enemy.

2   In order to carry out an attack, we must have means available. The material for raising fire should always be kept in readiness.

3   There is a proper season for making attacks with fire, and special days for starting a conflagration.

4   The proper season is when the weather is very dry; the special days are those when the moon is in the constellations of the Sieve, the Wall, the Wing or the Cross-bar; for these four are all days of rising wind.

5   In attacking with fire, one should be prepared to meet five possible developments:

6   (1) When fire breaks out inside the enemy's camp, respond at once with an attack from without.

7   (2) If there is an outbreak of fire, but the enemy's soldiers remain quiet, bide your time and do not attack.

8   (3) When the force of the flames has reached its height, follow it up with an attack, if that is practicable; if not, stay where you are.

9   (4) If it is possible to make an assault with fire from without, do not wait for it to break out within, but deliver your attack at a favourable moment.

10   (5) When you start a fire, be to windward of it. Do not attack from the leeward.

11   A wind that rises in the daytime lasts long, but a night breeze soon falls.

12   In every army, the five developments connected with fire must be known, the movements of the stars calculated, and a watch kept for the proper days.

13   Hence those who use fire as an aid to the attack show intelligence; those who use water as an aid to the attack gain an accession of strength.

14   By means of water, an enemy may be intercepted, but not robbed of all his belongings.

15   Unhappy is the fate of one who tries to win his battles and succeed in his attacks without cultivating the spirit of enterprise; for the result is waste of time and general stagnation.

16   Hence the saying: The enlightened ruler lays his plans well ahead; the good general cultivates his resources.

17   Move not unless you see an advantage; use not your troops unless there is something to be gained; fight not unless the position is critical.

18   No ruler should put troops into the field merely to gratify his own spleen; no general should fight a battle simply out of pique.

19   If it is to your advantage, make a forward move; if not, stay where you are.

20   Anger may in time change to gladness; vexation may be succeeded by content.

21   But a kingdom that has once been destroyed can never come again into being; nor can the dead ever be brought back to life.

22   Hence the enlightened ruler is heedful, and the good general full of caution. This is the way to keep a country at peace and an army intact.

Successful Problem Solving

Harnessing the prevailing winds of commerce will lend to a business considerable advantage. If a rival is already under the cosh and this looks set to continue, harsh as it may sound, the weather is set fair to pile on the pressure.

This could present the optimum time to launch a new breakthrough product or service to an audience schooled to be excited by disruption; to appeal to the market's pocket with super-competitive pricing that cannot be matched; or to initiate a major advertising campaign that floods the customer's senses and works to drown out any other messages.

The Firefighting Analogy

As well as raising profile and bringing the feel-good factor to one's own brand, in parallel, such actions implicitly draw the spotlight on to the competition's shortcomings, which will be unable to introduce anything new to the table, pre-occupied as it will be with fighting fires.

The Art of War gives over an entire chapter to attack by fire and illustrates the importance Sun Tzu attaches to manoeuvring the opposition into a state of emergency and keeping it there. It is an approach that will

afford unencumbered freedom of movement to establish and consolidate a position, since the competition will be in no position to engage.

Just as it was for the generals in Sun Tzu's time, so it is important for today's business leader not to be too lenient in such situations, since the art of war requires a capacity to be commercially merciless. So long as one has avoided travelling no-through roads of questionable legality, responsibility for a rival company finding itself in danger of going under ultimately falls on that firm and its leadership, its modus operandi, and the decisions it did and did not take.

It is not for the leader to help keep another company afloat, and to do so would be to do a disservice to one's own stakeholders. The laws of commerce are as the laws of nature in that 'survival of the fittest' is the principle which applies; ergo, it is perfectly natural that a weak company incapable of adaptation to its environment should cease to exist in that form.

Stirring up conflict with incendiary rhetoric is a modern day means of deploying fire as a weapon, and just as Sun Tzu has no misgivings about campaigning in this manner, so too must the modern leader be prepared to mix up a 'play nice' strategy with a salvo of attacks that has the opposition feeling the heat and wrestling with poor market visibility, leaving its customers exposed for the taking. We are left in no doubt as to Sun Tzu's thinking on such matters, given that he writes, 'When the force of the flames has reached its height, follow it up with an attack.'

That said, when it comes to playing with fire, it pays to be watchful, since it is an unpredictable beast and there exists the ever-present danger of the fire consuming one's own operation if a company gets too closely embroiled. For example, if making accusations of impropriety, a firm had better be sure its own house is in order and squeaky clean, since the market does not look kindly upon hypocrisy. It is why Sun Tzu says, 'When you start a fire, be to windward of it. Do not attack from the leeward.'

Avoiding Hypocrisy

Corporate hypocrisy is especially evident these days in some of the largest firms' ESG declarations or statements of intent, with certain companies appearing to believe their own press that they are implementing green business practices that purportedly minimize environmental impact, when, in fact, it amounts to little more than spin and hyperbole.

Generational disconnect can compound the problem, whereby older, out of touch executives may underestimate the media savviness, zeal and impactful quality of an increasingly disaffected global youth. This sees them overseeing an inflation of the truth that positions the firm as more progressive, responsible and caring than other players in the field, and so worthy of consumer or shareholder backing in the type of PR exercise that likely served the company well in years past. Yet, with increasingly high-profile grass roots movements placing multinationals under the highest scrutiny, this is a dangerous road to take and leaves firms super-exposed to having their corporate fingers burned.

Transparency, accountability and responsibility are no longer a 'nice to have' – rather, they constitute baseline expectations. Woe betide the executive that doesn't comprehend the new and permanent business reality that has stakeholders placing ever greater importance on natural capital.

A Network of Adjutants

To solve a problem cannot be done alone. While the leader has the final say, he or she relies on an army of enterprising subordinates to help enlighten them and nourish and grow the company with new thinking. Recognizing and nurturing potential is the mark of a fine leader, and it's a wise boss that brings clearly talented individuals into the fold before

they have a chance to establish a rival power base outside the circle of trust. Sun Tzu understands this when he writes that 'the good general cultivates his resources.'

In asserting that the leader should, 'Move not unless you see an advantage; use not your troops unless there is something to be gained; fight not unless the position is critical,' *The Art of War* is very clear that the gaining of an edge must lie behind all actions taken, and that to engage without rationale risks wasting resources for no benefit. As such, the nature, source and crux of a problem retarding progress towards a recognized objective must first be identified.

There is, for example, no point in a company subjecting a fellow operative in the marketplace to an intense firestorm of controversy if it poses little or no threat and operates in different commercial territory. Such an approach would be wasteful, as resources would need to be deployed to engage the company and manage the fallout for significantly less return than if they were allocated elsewhere.

Sun Tzu states that, 'No ruler should put troops into the field merely to gratify his own spleen; no general should fight a battle simply out of pique.'

We can take from this that to assist in establishing a rationale for action, and to temper any personal agendas, fleeting emotions or confirmation bias that may creep into their decision-making, the leader can and should rely on the network of company adjutants they have to hand. These in-house assets must be put to work to reconnoitre the market and secure the requisite information needed to inform the executive call that will determine the way forward.

Moreover, if a competitor is deemed such a threat that it warrants engagement, this suggests it may be worthy of acquiring or merging with. As such, it is important for a leader to ask oneself the value of raining fire and brimstone on a target like this, such that it serves to destroy any worth or usefulness it may hold for the future. As Sun Tzu states, 'a

kingdom that has once been destroyed can never come again into being; nor can the dead ever be brought back to life.'

These words perfectly encapsulate the central tenet of Sun Tzu's teaching that the best fights are the ones we avoid.

CHAPTER THIRTEEN

THE USE OF SPIES

用 間

1   Sun Tzu said: Raising a host of a hundred thousand men and marching them great distances entails heavy loss on the people and a drain on the resources of the State. The daily expenditure will amount to a thousand ounces of silver. There will be commotion at home and abroad, and men will drop down exhausted on the highways. As many as seven hundred thousand families will be impeded in their labour.

2   Hostile armies may face each other for years, striving for the victory which is decided in a single day. This being so, to remain in ignorance of the enemy's condition simply because one grudges the outlay of a hundred ounces of silver in honours and emoluments, is the height of inhumanity.

3   One who acts thus is no leader of men, no present help to his sovereign, no master of victory.

4   Thus, what enables the wise sovereign and the good general to strike and conquer, and achieve things beyond the reach of ordinary men, is foreknowledge.

5   Now this foreknowledge cannot be elicited from spirits; it cannot be obtained inductively from experience, nor by any deductive calculation.

6   Knowledge of the enemy's dispositions can only be obtained from other men.

7   Hence the use of spies, of whom there are five classes:

(1) Local spies;

(2) inward spies;

(3) converted spies;

(4) doomed spies;

(5) surviving spies.

8   When these five kinds of spy are all at work, none can discover the secret system. This is called 'divine manipulation of the threads'. It is the sovereign's most precious faculty.

9   Having local spies means employing the services of the inhabitants of a district.

10   Having inward spies, means making use of officials of the enemy.

11   Having converted spies, means getting hold of the enemy's spies and using them for our own purposes.

12   Having doomed spies, doing certain things openly for purposes of deception, and allowing our spies to know of them and report them to the enemy.

13   Surviving spies, finally, are those who bring back news from the enemy's camp.

14   Hence it is that with none in the whole army are more intimate relations to be maintained than with spies. None should be more liberally rewarded. In no other business should greater secrecy be preserved.

15   Spies cannot be usefully employed without a certain intuitive sagacity.

16 They cannot be properly managed without benevolence and straightforwardness.

17 Without subtle ingenuity of mind, one cannot make certain of the truth of their reports.

18 Be subtle! be subtle! and use your spies for every kind of business.

19 If a secret piece of news is divulged by a spy before the time is ripe, he must be put to death together with the man to whom the secret was told.

20 Whether the object be to crush an army, to storm a city, or to assassinate an individual, it is always necessary to begin by finding out the names of the attendants, the aides-de-camp, and door-keepers and sentries of the general in command. Our spies must be commissioned to ascertain these.

21 The enemy's spies who have come to spy on us must be sought out, tempted with bribes, led away and comfortably housed. Thus they will become converted spies and available for our service.

22 It is through the information brought by the converted spy that we are able to acquire and employ local and inward spies.

23   It is owing to his information, again, that we can cause the doomed spy to carry false tidings to the enemy.

24   Lastly, it is by his information that the surviving spy can be used on appointed occasions.

25   The end and aim of spying in all its five varieties is knowledge of the enemy; and this knowledge can only be derived, in the first instance, from the converted spy. Hence it is essential that the converted spy be treated with the utmost liberality.

26   Of old, the rise of the Yin dynasty was due to I Chih who had served under the Hsia. Likewise, the rise of the Chou dynasty was due to Lu Ya who had served under the Yin.

27   Hence it is only the enlightened ruler and the wise general who will use the highest intelligence of the army for purposes of spying and thereby they achieve great results. Spies are a most important element in warfare, because on them depends an army's ability to move.

Business Intelligence

The wisest leaders know that information is king when it comes to achieving victory swiftly and at minimum possible outlay. In Sun Tzu's day this meant the use of spies. Nowadays, it's business intelligence, which can provide precious insights into and an upper hand over the competition in today's no less bruising but rather more regulated corporate battlefield.

Balancing the Books

Sun Tzu begins his final chapter with the sobering words: 'Raising a host of a hundred thousand men and marching them great distances entails heavy loss on the people and a drain on the resources of the State.'

While there may be no glory in balancing the books, the leader underestimates its importance at their peril, and must recognize that long-drawn-out conflict is their enemy in this regard. The very best of them understand there is no better preparation for a fight – nothing, in fact, providing greater certainty of outcome – than gathering and making use of all legally obtainable business intelligence. Utilizing the right sort of knowledge means quick wins are there for the taking, thereby avoiding a situation where, 'Hostile armies may face each other for years, striving for the victory which is decided in a single day.'

Forsake Foreknowledge at Your Peril

Just like opponents on the battlefield, in commerce, material information that may afford advantage will not be gifted or given up easily. The takeaway here is to keep one's plans and thinking as closely guarded a secret as possible, because that's what the competition will be doing.

Furthermore, while inferences can be made as to the competition's likely trajectory and intentions from publicly held or legally acquired data, forward looking statements, anecdotal evidence, as well as the leader's own instinct and experience, must all be taken with a pinch of salt. While each resource is important, they remain cumulatively insufficient to generate the level of foreknowledge needed to strike on the course of action that will virtually guarantee victory.

In short, nothing beats intelligence-gathering boots on the ground seeking out reliable primary sources of information.

A certain Chinese military strategist knew this only too well, as illustrated when he writes, 'Now this foreknowledge cannot be elicited from spirits; it cannot be obtained inductively from experience, nor by any deductive calculation.'

Meanwhile, he goes on to say, 'Knowledge of the enemy's dispositions can only be obtained from other men.'

Keep One's Own Counsel

Of course, this begs the question of whether the other side are at it too. The answer is 'yes', and thus, one needs to be alert to whom one is speaking and keep one's own counsel on the important stuff. For just as in life there are gossip-hungry acquaintances within one's social circle that possess a knack for coaxing personal information out of us that we had no intention of giving up, so too these folk exist in business,

and their easy charm and apparent trustworthiness are highly prized qualities.

These figures can take many forms: journalists, employees, conference delegates, students, academics, or even a member at the golf club who strikes up a conversation, so it pays for the leader to be careful about what they divulge and to whom, and to communicate this to other holders of sensitive information within the top ranks.

While it has become de rigueur for most companies to ask their employees to sign non-disclosure agreements and to see to it they are contractually bound not to share, record, download or otherwise remove company information from approved locations, this is a fiendishly difficult area to police.

Given as much, it makes sense to avoid the problem in the first place by limiting individuals' access to 'need-to-know' only. Because the fewer people that know something, the harder it will be for any miscreants to get away with passing it to hostile actors undetected. It is also essential for the leader at the top – often the one figure that has access-all-areas status – to be mindful of the fact it is they that presents by far the biggest risk to the company's fortunes, given the extent of the critical information they hold, and that they are bound by the same overarching covenant to safeguard that which they know as anyone else at the firm.

Sword and Shield

One should, however, not be shy in making use of competitive intelligence tactics, so long as these are within the confines of the law and stakeholders privy to them will not consider them unethical as to be to the detriment of the company.

It is worth remembering here that what may not be permissible in one territory may be fair game in another. Either way, before undertaking

any activities in this area, a company will need to perform thorough due diligence to determine whether its potential strategy falls within an acceptable 'competitive intelligence' category or rather, the wrong side of the law. Unlike in Sun Tzu's day, the penalties for calling it wrong can be career-ending and company-ruining.

With corporate espionage involving taking proprietary or operational information such as customer datasets or marketing strategies, or the acquiring of intellectual property such as information on processes unique to a particular firm, this is serious stuff that can bring with it huge advantage. The temptation for bad actors is obvious to see, so the leader needs to be rigorous in creating the conditions to resist such advances.

To protect against such malign behaviour, it pays to have discoveries, designs and inventions fully patented and to keep a beady eye on critical data and those that make use of it. For those thinking such measures to be unnecessary and that legal recourse exists to right any wrongs visited upon a company in this area, it's worth remembering that if the source of the problem is traced back to a hostile foreign country, the chances of satisfaction will be less than zero. There will be no day in court, no compensation and critical trade secrets will have been lost; potentially to be sold to the highest bidder.

Ironically, despite taking a dim view of it within their own borders, nations both big and small are, to varying degrees, themselves engaged in state sponsored economic espionage, pulling out the trump card that this is to promote and protect national security interests. Sun Tzu would have approved.

It is essential that intelligence gatherers are appropriately recompensed, since what they bring to the table can mean the difference between victory and defeat. It is small wonder, for example, that investment analysts are so well remunerated, because those few that get it consistently right can make others very rich.

Such clever modern-day spies are an invaluable asset and as *The Art of War* notes in this matter, 'Hence it is that with none in the whole army are more intimate relations to be maintained than with spies. None should be more liberally rewarded. In no other business should greater secrecy be preserved.'

Handle with Care

At the same time, it is important to be on one's guard, since the very same qualities one makes use of to garner sufficient evidence to make a valid conjecture about a rival's situation and plans ahead of taking action, can also be redirected to one's own door. Consequently, any information proffered should always be cross-referenced, for *The Art of War* makes clear, 'Without subtle ingenuity of mind, one cannot make certain of the truth of their reports.'

Just as in Sun Tzu's day, the psychological make-up of those characters acting purely in self-interest rather than for the team gives to them the condition of guns for hire, while their clandestine nature, thrill-seeking inclinations and sense of entitlement can make for a maverick asset that must be handled with care.

That said, the value of first-hand accounts of what's going on in enemy territory should not be sniffed at. Today, new employees with experience of working for the competition can bring with them important insights, as well as, potentially, a bulging contacts book and new business, subject to this not being in breach of any non-compete terms and conditions their old employer has released them under and with which they and their new paymasters are bound to comply.

These new recruits are likely to come armed with a potent competitive zeal linked to a desire to validate the job move by helping their new employer outperform their old organization. However, it will exist in a

latent form and so first needs to be delicately drawn out before it can be made use of.

As such, it is in the leader's best interests to help those in question manage and motivate the psychological shift that needs to happen in advance of the new hire transferring their sense of belonging as smoothly and swiftly as possible to one's organization, and so put to bed any emotional conflict of interest they may be feeling.

This is laid out in one of *The Art of War*'s closing passages, where Sun Tzu explains that, 'The end and aim of spying in all its...varieties is knowledge of the enemy; and this knowledge can only be derived, in the first instance, from the converted spy.'

Be Humble

Sun Tzu rounds off his mini epic for the ages by talking of dynasties that survived due to the passing on of knowledge, and of leaders recognizing talent in others and putting it to best use for the greater good. Such approaches speak to enlightenment and wisdom, we are told.

Some two and a half thousand years may have passed, but the message that there is no place for ego-infused thinking or glory-seeking behaviour resonates as much in the modern business arena as it did back then on the battlefields of what we know today as China.

The corporate leader that thinks they know best; that overrides all the signs and signals from the past and present, is sure to damage or destroy that which they have been called upon to guard and grow.

He or she that embraces true humility, meanwhile, is set up for success.

Epilogue

The settings may be very different and over two millennia apart, but just like the revered religious texts collated in remote corners of the globe have withstood the ages to transcend place and time to inspire worldwide devotion, so too the messages contained within Sun Tzu's *The Art of War* burn brighter today than ever.

So how could a short treatise seemingly concerned with military strategy speak to us so profoundly across the aeons?

That its messages have proved so enduring is because they talk to eternal truths that are as readily applicable to today's modern business landscape as to the ancient Chinese battlefields.

While the sands of custom, convention and procedure may be ever-shifting, people are people, as ever they were, exhibiting the same strengths and fallibilities; the same light and dark traits today as when *The Art of War* made its first appearance.

Moreover, in the figure of Sun Tzu, we have no ordinary author.

If this were just a military man writing, we'd have a dry handbook on combat manoeuvres that would have no business resonating outside of those circles. Similarly, the strategist would solely be drawing our attention to plans and directions, and while no doubt ingenious for the time, these would of themselves have little of interest to say to us today. And, as for Sun Tzu, the philosopher, if this were the only hat he wore, though sure to interest scholars, it's highly unlikely an ancient Chinese

credo without context would be considered to have any real-world application in the 21st century.

Rather, the concise but mighty tome's stellar quality and reverberance through space and time is down to the fact that Sun Tzu was all of these things. At one and the same time: writer, general, strategist and philosopher.

Sun Tzu fuses his skill sets to deliver something wholly unique – a compact epic that blends legend with fact, logic with feeling, poetry with prose to elevate *The Art of War* to more than the sum of its words; to exist in a separate state of profound truth and permanence.

Cumulatively, the text shows the writer's perspicacity and uncanny ability to penetrate that which is confusing and obscured, where he lifts the mist and brings order to the chaos of the human condition to create an iconic piece of work. And, like all the best works, it aspires to be nothing, yet effortlessly achieves.

That it was crafted so long ago is part of the secret of its enduring charm. Its very durability and tried and tested formulae are why it is so trusted. In a world where everyone's broadcasting, yet precious few listening, this is what allows it to shine through the white noise, bringing to it a quality guarantee for business leaders seeking guidance from a source without an agenda.

And because Sun Tzu is long dead and has no estate benefiting from a carefully curated brand, there can be no agenda. This is very reassuring.

However, with profound shifts in attitudes unprecedentedly transforming the look and feel of Western society and finding expression in the marketplace, could the relevance of Sun Tzu's words soon be on the wane? What value or application could ancient declarations from a far-off place and time possibly have for today's corporate chiefs increasingly wrestling with how best to speak sincerely and convincingly to a diverse 'just be yourself' world?

Is it conceivable *The Art of War* could still be occupying pride of place

on the business bookshelves in another two and a half thousand years?

There are good reasons to think so. And that is because, regardless of the threats faced, the technological advances made, or the waxing and waning fortunes of progressives and traditionalists, the human condition is a constant and it is these characteristics, limitations and experiences that Sun Tzu's writing speaks to – and which business leaders crave insights into.

It in no way diminishes the capacity of Sun Tzu's writings to deliver enlightenment if today's leaders are held to account in a way he could scarcely have comprehended or that diversity and inclusion have become essential watchwords for any chief that wants to get on. Because, while it would be a stretch to imagine Sun Tzu from ancient China flying the flag for accountability or equality of opportunity, given the rigid parameters of the world in which he existed, in transposing his writings to today's business landscape we can certainly acknowledge his underlying advocacy for that which would enhance efficiency.

The Art of War talks of the need to recognize talent and reward achievement. However, it's clear that many of today's glass ceiling company hierarchies are preventing this from happening at scale, meaning the firms in question are placing themselves at needless disadvantage. If customers are demanding a more compassionate and empathetic approach from companies in return for their business, it seems singularly self-defeating to pack a boardroom exclusively with men drawn from a narrow demographic.

With *The Art of War* underpinned throughout by promotion of the precept that the 'supreme art of war is to subdue the enemy without fighting', those engaged in passive resistance to oppression today would appear to be channelling just such a message. A refusal to comply with requirements at scale in collective non-violent opposition to authority can prove to be a highly effective driver of change and marries beautifully with the notion that the best fights are the ones we avoid.

Of course, protests can be violently quelled by those that would seek to preserve the status quo that has served them so well, but at other times they can act to usher in no less than a new dawn in history. The trick – as *The Art of War* makes clear – is to know the enemy, know one's objectives, and know one's limits.

The same is true for the leader. The best of them will know when they are no longer up to the job and it's time to make way for new blood. In early 2023, both New Zealand Prime Minister, Jacinda Ardern, and Scottish First Minister, Nicola Sturgeon did just that in quick succession. The former acknowledged she no longer had enough in the tank, while the latter admitted to the adverse physical and mental impact of occupying the role long term, such that she did not feel able to continue to discharge her duties to a satisfactory standard.

These rare displays of humanity from individuals wielding such a level of authority speaks to a profound *Art of War*-like understanding that leadership is service not mastery and will hopefully light the way for other leaders under stress.

In politics, as in business, all the ingredients are present for the leader to be in a constant state of agitation if they are not able to exercise emotional control and maintain constant mental focus. And while *The Art of War* explains what one needs to do to be an effective leader, at the same time it recognizes leadership is an all-consuming calling that requires one to be forever alert to opponents' manoeuvres, to anticipate their next move and to make decisions on how best to parry any blows.

Sun Tzu's work also talks of the need to 'know yourself', and so the ability for a leader to recognize when their time is up is surely the perfect modern-day expression of this and speaks to having reached a profound level of self-insight. Equally, *The Art of War* would have no time for the leader that stayed in post despite having lost focus, thereby jeopardizing the fortunes of the army – in this case, the New Zealand and Scottish electorates.

The societal conventions of the time are irrelevant to the efficacy of *The Art of War* to continue to speak to us, in the same way many believers do not reject the underlying messages in religious texts just because some of the ancient contexts are wildly at odds with current codes. In fact, one only has to look back a few years to see how swiftly conventions change.

Sun Tzu's text is concerned with spiritual awakening and renewal, emotion, aspiration, learning, reflection, conflict, morality, of how people behave towards each other and themselves. In other words, timeless preoccupations made manifest on the battlegrounds of business.

In a world of endless interfaces and existential threats, there is probably more need for *The Art of War*'s wisdom and enlightenment than ever before. Today's corporate leader has to process an almost overwhelming number of dynamics in order to successfully position their company for the people, for the planet and at the same time for profit. It is no small task.

Even some of the most seemingly formidable CEOs are leaving roles or taking time out due to stress, depression or extreme exhaustion. Others are desperate for help, but such is the aura of resilience they have traditionally had to project, they are reluctant to share their struggles. In Sun Tzu's mighty yet mini tome can be found clues for keeping on top of it all.

Life expectancy and quality of life expectations are markedly higher than they were when *The Art of War* was written, yet modern life is not delivering. Conflict may not be of the military variety for most these days, but the personal battles are many and raging – both with others and with oneself. And so, for all the apparent advances, today's business leader is seemingly no better at planning, assessing, negotiating, engaging in healthy functional competition, forming mutually respectful relationships or exercising humility than they were even before Sun Tzu's time.

But it's not a hopeless situation. Help is out there if one wants it. The majority will think they know best and eschew any assistance, but

as they have throughout history, the humble will seek out *The Art of War*'s wisdom and use it as both a springboard and constant compass to go on a lifelong voyage of discovery. This zeal to better themselves and to improve their lot and that of others, will see enlightenment spill into every corner of their lives.

These are the ones that will become tomorrow's great leaders the eternal herd will look to be guided by.

For today's business leaders, the fight to come is going to be as much about navigating and managing evolving relations with primary stakeholders, like customers, employees, shareholders, investors and the wider community in which their companies operate, as it will be the competition. But, while this may sound like a more benevolent battlefield, ever higher expectations and increasingly exacting demands will mean the leader's job is sure to be as complex as ever, and the need for *The Art of War*'s words of wisdom just as great.

Index

INDEX